Rock Bottom
To
The Being Behind
The Face

By
Jim Lowitz

Leaning Rock Press
Gales Ferry, CT

Copyright © 2026, Jim Lowitz

All rights reserved. No parts of this publication may be reproduced, stored in a database or retrieval system, or transmitted, in any form or by any means, without the prior permission of the author or publisher except by a reviewer who may quote brief passages in a review.

Leaning Rock Press
Gales Ferry, CT 06335
leaningrockpress@gmail.com
www.leaningrockpress.com

978-1-960596-90-1, Hardcover
978-1-960596-91-8, Softcover

Library of Congress Control Number: 2026905353

Publisher's Cataloging-in-Publication Data
(Prepared by Cassidy Cataloguing's PCIP Service)

Names: Lowitz, Jim, author.
Title: Rock bottom to the being behind the face / by Jim Lowitz.
Description: Identifiers: ISBN: 9781960596901 (hardcover) | 9781960596918 (softcover)
Subjects: LCSH: Lowitz, Jim--Religion. | Spirituality. | Meditation. | Religions. | Mindfulness (Psychology) | Self-realization. | Change (Psychology) | LCGFT: Autobiographies. | BISAC: MIND, BODY, SPIRIT / Ayurveda. | MIND, BODY, SPIRIT / Mindfulness & Meditation. | BIOGRAPHY & AUTOBIOGRAPHY / Memoirs.
Classification: LCC: BL624 .L69 2026 | DDC: 204.4--dc23

Dedication

This was written to my 8-year-old self, who knew there was more to this life than was visible and knew that one day, when he was older, he would understand. It was also written to my 88-year-old self, who waits to see what I have become.

Table of Contents

Remembering Preciousness

When I began my spiritual path in study and practice, the concept and lofty goal and drive to connect to God, (The Creator. The Infinite Eternal Mind, Hashem, Atum, Great Spirit, The Supreme Being Self, Wakan Tanka, Ein Soph, whatever name you wish to use) was not my objective. It was inconceivable. I wanted to improve in a new agey "body, mind and spirit" kind of way. Mostly body, since I was in my early twenties and was very into building my body and my business. I wanted to be a fully rounded successful young man and looking the part was obsessive to me, and.... I wanted to attract women!

As I consider the concept of " Realization of God", the highest knowing- that I am a portion of The All, The Creator, I celebrate that I have received this knowing, and I hope to convey how this miracle in my life occurred. I am struck by the time that has passed and all the work I was guided to do to accept this knowledge.

There are, in my experience, 2 important aspects to Awareness and Realization of God. The first part I have described as a unique knowing that I am a portion of the Creator and a part of existence. I have always been and always will be, in some form beyond time and space. A self within and part of the One Self. A singularity within the multiplicity of The All.

The Realization of God is the ultimate goal of human life according to Hinduism. It is the realization that the individual soul (Atman) is identical to the divine universal spirit (Brahman)

This knowing can only be attained by direct experience and I am grateful for this experience and I have written in detail about my experiences in this knowing.

The second part of this realization is that I am / we are so very precious to The Creator and all those Others serving The Holy one. We are loved more than we can possibly feel in this 3rd dimensional human body. I have experienced this precious love and I hope to convey this feeling that I have felt so that you can receive some portion of what I know to be true.

There is a deja vu in all of this. It is a remembering- not a new experience- its the understanding that I now remember this Precious Love and that this life has always been for me, about remembering and experiencing the Precious Love the Creator has for all of us.

Jim Lowitz, Dec 2025

Prologue

The Veil Begins To Tear

It was 3 am in the morning when it happened, one of those hours when sleep shifted into an abrupt waking- I had fallen asleep and certainly was not thinking about the book.

Then, my left hand began its familiar shake, followed by heat and numbness. This shaking and throbbing numbness had started first about 20 years ago. It was subtle at first. My left thumb would go numb when a profound truth was thought or I said a truth or I heard a spiritual truth spoken or I was meditating. But now, it has become something extraordinary. My entire hand and wrist pulsed with an electric throbbing,tingling and numbness that vibrated and shook. It was never painful, but it was powerful and impossible to ignore when awakened in such a way.

Eventually, as the vibration spread through my entire hand and then into my wristband forearm, it would jolt me out of a deep sleep.

I immediately knew this was not some kind of illness.This was a signal. It was time to receive a communication. It is always the left hand. Always the unmistakable vibration. It reminded me of the Plant Medicine Ceremonies as the energy arrives and work begins. But, this happens now without medicine in the body. This is something very different. A form of communication signal that required only my willingness and my attention to what would follow next. At night when this frequency arrived, I understood.

I was fully awake, yet I had not moved. My eyes were closed, but I could see. My third eye is open now. Everything was purple hues, like clouds slowly clearing until my entire visual field glowed with this majestic single color. They were writing one word at a time:

"JIMMY, THIS IS YOU." An arrow, curved to the left pointing to a stick figure sitting at a desk with a pen in hand and a book on the desk.

Then, they wrote this:

"When will you start writing again?"

I had stopped writing for many months with writers' block. It was now clear. I needed to finish this book.

PART 1

FOUNDATIONS AND EARLY SPIRITUAL AWAKENING

Chapter 1

The Call Beneath The Surface

I remember watching *The Greatest Story Ever Told* as a child, sitting with my family and taking in the grand, ancient stories on the screen. Growing up in a Reform Jewish home, I always had a natural curiosity about spiritual figures from different traditions. To me, figures like Jesus or Buddha were fascinating not as a challenge to my beliefs but as an invitation to wonder who they might have been and what their stories meant to so many people.

In our family household Jesus was often seen simply as a wise teacher from another path. I suspected there was much more to the man. Even from a young age, I found myself intrigued by the idea that different traditions hold different pieces of a much larger puzzle. That curiosity and drive has stayed with me all of my life becoming my own spiritual path. It has guided me to explore, question always with a sense of respect for the many paths that so many of us walk.

It was a complicated and difficult childhood. My father was a well-known surgeon in Baltimore. My mother was diagnosed with breast cancer at just 36 years old, with four children aged 6 to 13. She was given nine months to live when first diagnosed, and it devastated my father, as you would expect.

A doctor friend of my father, Irv, told me he was there at the time of the diagnosis. When my father got the news about Sonia, he leaned his 6'1" athletic body against the hospital wall, crying loudly and painfully. From that moment on, our family life changed.

My mother transformed her cancer into a career. Her cancer and all the treatments became the backdrop of our childhood. In many ways, this shaped all four of us, including me.

We didn't complain much when it came to injuries or anything like that. We had to be tough because my mother was the toughest person I've ever known.

Once, I was teasing my younger brother while he was doing his homework, and he took his pencil and stabbed me in the arm. The pencil point went in and snapped off, with about three inches of the pencil still stuck outside of my arm. Quite a sight.

My mother was taking a bath, and I knocked on the door and said, "Mom, John stabbed me in the arm, and the pencil is sticking out, and there's blood coming down."

My mother said, "Jimmy, I'm in the bath and I'll be out in 20 minutes."

That should give you an idea of what I mean when I say it was a difficult upbringing, and you learned toughness. I waited for her to get out of the bathroom. My father was in the emergency room and looked at my arm with the 3 inches of pencil sticking out of my arm and said it calmly as can be, "Let's see... huh! It's deeper there than I thought." He took it out, put some stitches in, and I still have the scar.

Our house was filled with books and with a belief: If you studied and used your mind diligently, your intellect would expand. My father described the brain as a muscle that must be exercised constantly through study and reading.

On Friday nights, we sat around the table for Shabbat dinner. If any subject was brought up and you had an opinion (believe me, you had to wait until you were at least ten or eleven years old before saying a word at that table), you had better come prepared with facts. My father would quietly listen to your opinion, then give you this look. He had a powerful face. And then he would say, "So that's your point? Well, look it up."

I would run upstairs, grab the encyclopedia, and search through it to find the subject matter and the proof to support my thinking. That might also mean grabbing the dictionary or thesaurus, and I would bring it down to the table, find pages to support the opinion/argument, and off we would go. Everybody (all 6 of us) was in a long discussion, while my mother and father sometimes exchanged a secret smile across the table. It was truly the Socratic method of learning. A question is asked, and knowledge and learning follow with more questions and more learning.

My parents had passion, and sometime`s that passion turned into horrible arguments. There was a cloud at times over the house, and we had to walk on eggshells. I learned about the reactive mind just from watching my parents respond to each other and each one of us, and that later became a theme in my own development.

I now believe that if the Buddhists are right, and we choose our soul groups and parents to travel with through physical lifetimes, then we are choosing their flaws as well as their teachings. These experiences help us transform, elevate, and grow.

On my 8th birthday, I left the house and walked across the street to the elementary school where we played tag in the mornings before class. I stood on one of the grates on the tarred playground that served as home base and said to myself, "I don't know why I am saying this, but there is more to this life than this, and one day when I'm older, I will understand." I made a vow to remember that moment, because something in me knew it was important.

Each birthday since then, I still see that little eight-year-old boy's face. And now, finally, I understand exactly what he, what I meant.

When I think about that boy, I remember the questions I asked as I grew older, and the ones I eventually answered as I became more aware. "What is space? What is time?" Later, I asked the same questions that Thoth once posed: "What is God? What is reality?"

The answers I received are true messages and insights that I now hope you will find meaningful.

As I write the story of my path, the questions keep coming: If you had time, where would you put it? If you had space, where would it be? Who created time and space? These questions inspired me to begin my studies, which I later understood to be mysticism. So, at the age of 23, I began to frequent what we called "new age bookstores", explore meditation, and accept that this was my true passion.

One example of what I learned is the paradox of time. The present moment, or "the now," sits between two measures that do not exist: the past and the future. The past does not exist BECAUSE IT'S GONE, and the future is yet to come, SO IT DOES NOT EXIST; therefore, time is a paradox and does not exist, at least not as we imagine it.

The only logical understanding of time I came to accept is that it is an Eternal Now, with the past and future folded into it. Time must be simultaneous. Our belief in a linear past, present, and future is based on our brain's limited interpretation of reality. For us, time is simply the orderly separation of events.

By my mid thirties, I was a businessman with more than a hundred people working in my insurance lead marketing company. I had already sold an impaired risk and disability insurance agency, so the entrepreneurial spirit in me had been realized. Business was going well. My wife and I had designed and built a beautiful house in the countryside. Our son and daughter were born over the next five years and brought us great joy. But we also suffered great losses.

My spiritual path was put on hold for many years. My father-in-law and my mother died within a year of each other. My beloved dog died a few months later. Then, five years later, my father passed away. By the time I was 45 years old, both my parents and my father-in-law were all gone. It is important to support those around you when grieving. My childhood with my mother's illness seemed to have seamlessly intertwined with my adult young life.

Grief has a way of leading you in other directions, but I was to learn that real suffering can be, and often is, transformative. My mother was a beautiful woman who faced death at just 36 due to breast cancer. With less than a year of life expectancy, she did not curl up in despair.

It became clear that she had an extraordinarily fighting spirit. She helped to found Reach to Recovery, a branch of the American Cancer Society. Its mission was to work with mastectomy and breast cancer patients independently of hospitals, focusing on a woman-to-woman support system. She even designed their logo.

The idea of women entering hospitals to help the new patients after breast cancer surgery outraged the medical establishment. My father, Irv, became my mother's strongest advocate. Little by little, they created an army of thousands of volunteers who provided the emotional support that their doctors were not providing.

As a young boy, I witnessed so much trauma and strength that it was both inspiring and difficult. Sonia was always on a new drug for cancer, and always worried. We grew up in a world of unknown health outcomes, and the pressure was evident on my parents' faces when they spoke.

My sister, brothers, and I all agreed that our mother was extraordinarily unshakable. She defied her prognosis and taught our family powerful lessons about life. My parents were soulmates.

Sonia, six years old, had blond hair, green eyes, and a huge crush on an athletic boy from the neighborhood. That boy was Irv. He was 17 at the time, always walking around with a football, baseball, or basketball, and was a star goalie in soccer, a high school All-American. He barely noticed that his childhood friend Casey had a baby sister, Sonia, who was madly in crush with him.

Years later, my father served as an officer in the Navy during World War II. About ten years after that, he visited his friend Casey and saw Sonia, now seventeen, standing at the top of the stairs. Sonia and her mother looked at Irv in his Navy uniform, and Sonia told her mother, "I am going to marry him!"

My father saw Sonia and said to himself, "That's the most beautiful girl I've ever seen." He always added, "But I had to wait... she was only seventeen." My mother would always counter with a smile, "We didn't wait very long." My parents never hid their attraction for each other, which lasted a lifetime.

They were married when she was just 22, and they were a stunning couple. He was 6'1", 185 lbs., and the classic tall, dark, and handsome. She had blond hair, green eyes, a beautiful face, and a graceful figure.

They supported each other as powerful allies throughout their lives until she passed away at the age of 69. My father died of a broken heart five years later at 85. They said it was a heart attack, but his heart was attacked by grief.

My father used to come over to my house for Friday night dinners. He always talked about Sonia and cried. It was very difficult to witness and experience the depth of his pain.

Then something very strange occurred one year after my mother died. He stopped crying and never mentioned Sonia again. He talked about his soccer days at the University of MD, College Park, and only talked about high school and college, but never mentioned being a surgeon or any part of his life after marrying Sonia.

Finally, I understood. He had blocked out all memories of his life from the moment he married her, because he could not bear the pain.

This is what soulmates go through when one of them dies.

My brother had been estranged for a long time, but he came to my parents' house during those last few days, and they both needed that reconnection. All of us knew that my mother was very worried about whether my 80-year-old father would be okay after she was gone. He depended on her for so much.

We told my father that he needed to tell Sonia he would be all right, to give her permission to let go, but he hadn't said the words. They were too painful for him.

We were all surrounding her bed in their apartment when, suddenly, my mother gasped and her eyes opened wide, and her tongue that was hanging on the side of her mouth was in her now beautiful, unlined, luminous face. This was a supernatural event.

We had witnessed, for several days, her almost arguing with someone or something; there were no words, just murmurs and deep lines in her forehead. But now, her face looked perfect, and her green eyes had a color I had never seen before.

As I write this, I now understand the dimension she was visiting, but it was shocking, and each of us knew we had watched something supernatural. She had been in a coma for a week and had almost no pulse. My father's friend, who was also a doctor, would take Sonia's pulse, and we were alerted that it was feathery, virtually undetectable. That's when we knew she was just minutes away, and we all gathered around her bed.

Suddenly, my mother sat up in bed, grabbed my father by the neck, and gave him a full kiss on the lips. My father told her he would be okay and that he loved her. She then looked at each one of us, saying goodbye with her eyes, as we all began talking at once.

She took one longer glance at Irv, slowly lay back down, took one final breath, and SHE WAS GONE.

We all noticed an amber and green light in the room, even though it was dark outside. It was truly a surreal moment. My father was broken, as we all were, but none of us could stop talking about what we had just witnessed.

We all had a scotch together and gently cried together. We were all enthralled about the mysteries of life and death, and what we all saw in that apartment the night my mother died.

I said to my father, "Mom is going to visit you. Please let me know when she does." Irv never believed in supernatural things, but he had changed that night, and he just nodded that he would let me know. He asked me to stay with him that night, and we slept on the bed that Mom and Dad shared for 47 years. I know that Sonia appreciated that we comforted each other.

A few nights later, my father told me that she had visited him. She was wearing her favorite negligee and had a hugesmile on her face. He kept excitedly saying, "Can you believe it?"

Chapter 2

The First Openings

(Part 1)

My spiritual path took on a form of urgency. I would go to New Age stores and find literally everything I could on UFOs (I joined MUFON, the Mutual UFO Network), meditation and channeling, religions, and ancient civilizations. The further back the civilizations and the older the mythologies, the more interesting they were to me. I was always drawn to Lemuria/Mu, Atlantis, Khem, and the King's List going back hundreds of thousands of years.

As I look at it now, it's obvious to me that we haven't been told the full truth about our history as a civilization. If something didn't fit a certain belief system, the archaeology would be ignored or "debunked." Many believe that the pyramids were not built by the Egyptians 4,000 years ago but are much older. It has been shown that water erosion, not wind, caused the wear on certain structures. This would place the timeline at more than 11,000 years ago, during a time of heavy rain or possibly a deluge. That erosion simply could not have occurred during the period Egyptologists claim.[1] It points to a completely different civilization, and this fact has been hidden for too long. Science and spiritualism are not mutually exclusive; in fact, they are now beginning to blur.

Albert Einstein was once asked about a theory regarding the randomness of life and existence. His reply was, "God does not play dice."[2] The greatest mathematician (many consider having lived), Ramanujan, developed the equation for measuring infinity when

---

1. Dr. Robert M Schoch,Forgotten Civilization:"The roll of solar outbursts in our past and future",Inner Traditions,2012 pp 11-34
2. Albert Einstein, Hedwig Born and Max Born, The Born-Einstein Letters (Macmillan,1971, page 91)

no one at Oxford or Cambridge believed it possible.[3] He said his ideas came to him in dreams from God and a Hindu goddess. Tesla claimed that many of his theories in mathematics, engineering, and physics came from beings from other worlds.[4] It's interesting that some of the most brilliant minds in history leaned toward the idea of a planned existence rather than random chance.

Many of them understood that existence seems to have been thought into reality. Where did the elements of life, the stars, and the galaxies come from? Even if science can explain the Big Bang, it cannot explain the origin of time, space, or gravity. Science can't fully explain quantum entanglement, either, why or how electrons are connected. It makes more sense if we consider that there is One Mind. If the universe is one atom, of course, it would be entangled. There is no separation; that is the illusion. This universe was thought into existence by one supreme, all-knowing mind, so naturally it acts differently when observed. We create our own reality because we are part of that One Mind. It is us.

There is just One Mind, and we are apertures through which the universe experiences itself. We are singularities within the multiplicity of the infinite, eternal Mind. We are a monad. We are a sinusoidal wave. We are it. You are it.

My favorite poem from the Book of the Dead explains….

I am one feeling myself divided

I am 2 and 4, and 8

I am the universe in diversity

Here are my transformations

These are my selves coming together

This is my becoming one[5]

3. G. H. Hardy, Ramanujan:Twelve lectures on Subjects by his life and works, (Cambridge: Cambridge University Press, 1940)
4. Nikola Tesla, "My Inventions" Electrical Experiments Magazine,(1919) pp 16-17, https://archive.org/details/electricalexperi07gern/page/16/mode/2up
5. Unknown author, Wallis Budge (Translator) *The Egyptian Book of the Dead,* (Sirius, 2021)

The Creator of all existence, who used imagination to bring it forth, is beyond time and space. If the universe (or universes) was thought into existence with sound, light, frequency, and vibration, then this sound or words emanating from the Creator must be eternal. Eternity and infinity make sense if the Creator not only exists beyond time and space but also creates time and space to hold its thoughts.

When first considering the title of this book, "The Being Behind the Face," the title choice felt close to describing my path. But a very good friend felt it was incomplete. When I considered what else might be needed to convey my story, it came to me with certainty: Rock Bottom to The Being Behind the Face. My friend and teacher, Tolo, agreed immediately. He always said I should be a teacher and writer. My usual reply was, "Teach what, how to screw things up in my life?" He laughed and said, "Yes, of course! Who's not going to relate to you?

My mother gave me a Masonic ring when I was 21 years old. What is interesting about this is that it turns out I am most likely the only son or cousin who wanted to learn about Freemasonry and study it, so the ring ended up on my finger. I liked the look of the ring and wore it until I found out you're only supposed to wear the ring if you are a Master Mason. I continued to wear it, anyway, knowing that at some point soon I would become a Mason. I did become a Mason at age 27, and at 33 I was initiated as a 32nd degree Mason.

I will not get much into Masonry at this point in the story, but I will say that I was stunned to find out years later that there was a connection between the ancient Egyptians, the Land of Khem, Thoth, and Masonry.

I spent quite a bit of time in Sedona, two or three weeks per year, meditating with a group that soon became very close. When I first began to meditate, I couldn't do it for five minutes, but within a year or so, I found myself able to sit quietly for hours at a time. It was quite something, the very first time I realized I had been in that space for three hours.

What I learned from meditation is that it's not about getting control of thoughts or using your mind to "do" something; it's about quieting your mind. Meditation allows thoughts to come in and to simply observe them. You are the observer, and you are aware. At your essence, you are awareness. It was many years later when I truly understood what it felt to experience awareness - to know that this awareness is what I am..

It is said that praying is talking to God, and meditating is God talking to you. It was not until my first Ayahuasca experience that I truly experienced God, and it transformed me. The difference between belief and knowing became clear. Carl Jung said it best when asked if he still believed in God: "Believe? Do I still believe in God? That's a good question... I don't believe. I know."[6]

I studied Buddhism, including Zen Buddhism and Tibetan Buddhism, and was initiated into Nichiren Buddhism as well as Kriya Yoga. I have read many of Paramahamsa Yogananda's books.

I wear the prayer Om Mani Padme Hum on my wrist. It is the Dalai Lama's favorite chant and means that through wisdom and practice, I will have the thoughts, mind, and body of a Buddha.

I love Zen Buddhism for its powerful simplicity: "I am a drop of water in the ocean; therefore, I am the ocean." "I am a grain of sand in the desert; therefore, I am the desert. "I am a cell in the heart of God, therefore I am God.

Buddhism focuses on the Lotus Sutra, and the chant Nam Myoho Renge Kyo means that I dedicate myself to the mystical law (cause and effect).

Jesus said a few very simple and complete statements that I am drawn to: "Do unto others as you would have them do to you" (Mathew 7:12 and Luke 6:31), which is from the Torah. "Treat your neighbor as you would yourself"(Mark 12:29-30). "The kingdom of God is within." (Luke 17:20–21). His favorite prayer was the Shema: "Hear, O Israel, the Lord your God, the Lord is One. You shall love the Lord your God with all your heart, all your soul, and all your might." (Deuteronomy 6:4-5)

6. Carl Jung, Interview on BBC Television with John Freeman, (March 1959).

I studied Hinduism, which is well over 10,000 years old and most likely 20 or even 30,000 years old. I like so much of it, "Sat Chit Ananda": existence/being, consciousness, and bliss. Shiva, the destroyer; Vishnu, the preserver; and Brahma, the creator. We destroy the old to make room for the transformed you.

It is the oldest religion that we know of. I have enjoyed the disciplines and teachings in all the Eastern religions. In fact, I have taken pearls from all of them.

When I studied Kabbalah, I found an interesting synergy between Hinduism, Hermeticism, String Theory, and the understanding of the dimensions of reality and the formation of existence.

Buddhism taught that through suffering, the seeds of change begin. The Lotus Sutra describes the path of the lotus, which is the metaphor of life, that we must grow through the muck and mud, and all that darkness, before we can sprout into the beautiful flower that we are.

Apparently, for me, I needed to deconstruct everything about myself that I identified as me. In 2017, I was suffering. I was disgusted with my personality, my actions, my decisions, and my constant self-sabotage. I didn't realize I was doing this on a conscious level, but it was happening nonetheless. I was happily married (most of the time), reasonably successful in business, married to a beautiful, successful woman, and I was a "body, mind, and spirit guy" living in the house on the hill that we had built. At 35, most people said, "Jim, you have really made it." Sure. But why was I not happy? I had created everything I had written down and said aloud.

My destruction of my old self was done unconsciously, so it was rather simple, devastating, and surgical in its efficiency. Using manifestation magic is complicated; it manifests the good and the bad. All you must do is have a desire and a very strong emotional charge, and you will transform yourself. Most people just say, How did I get here? Why is this happening to me? They never imagined that they created it all. Thoughts are things; they are imagined and given energy and and emoted in sound and matter is created. I am, I create.

The first thing I did, unconsciously, was end my marriage and create self-loathing, regret, pain, and depression. The second thing I did was move to Florida to escape the blame and start a new life, leaving everyone in Baltimore, Maryland. I knew I was being judged, and I could feel the judgment. While everyone else, my ex-wife and the kids, had seamlessly moved on, I was left with self-loathing, judgment, and, most importantly, regret.

The third thing I did was to have a completely unnecessary L4–L5 fusion on a perfectly imperfect back. I thought this would make me more powerful and look my absolute best as a newly single man in Florida. Since this was all about deconstruction, I should've known the surgery would be less than successful. I ended up in bed for three months. I took so many naps that even my own dog would look at me and telepathically say, "Another nap?"

From age 18, I spent a great deal of time lifting weights and building a lean, defined body. I always had significant natural strength. By my mid-twenties, I had no problem benching 300 pounds and squatting 400 pounds.

In high school, my brother John was in my French class when I was a senior. He loved to tell the biggest dudes in the school that they could not beat his brother in arm wrestling. He would organize the strongest guys at Northwestern High School to arm wrestle me. They would line up outside the front door of French class, five or six guys ready to go.

My school was 85% African American; the athletes all knew me. I would walk down the hall and hear, "There's Lowitz." I was the only white guy on the track team. I won the state for JV in high jump, and as a senior, took third place in high jump at the MSA Championship, Maryland Scholastic Association. I had always had almost freakish strength, and none of those guys could ever beat me. I was about 155 pounds in high school, and some of these athletes were 100 lbs. heavier than me. I would tell them just to say when to start, and within five seconds the match was over, and the predictable – " I can't believe he beat me." Every time, five seconds.

I invested most of my energy in this identity of the body beautiful. I was 6% body fat on 6'1", 192 pounds. I seemed to have inherited the best genes from both my mother and father. Friends would say, "Jim, you hit the genetic lottery." I was always very fast and athletic. Most sports came easily to me. By fifteen, I could easily and accurately throw a football 55 to 65 yards in the air, and excelled in most sportsI tried, football, track and field, tennis, and baseball. I was a lifeguard in Ocean City, but it's fair to say I was not a great swimmer in the ocean. If you were drowning within 50 yards of the water, I would be fast to get to you. If you were further out...better call Saul.

So, here I was in my late 50s, laid up in bed with a poor surgical result that had changed my anatomy. I had physical pain to go with my self-loathing. Perfect. I was in mental and physical pain, and now I was taking hydrocodone for the physical pain. My beautiful, powerful body was racked with pain and anatomically changed.

I wasn't keeping an eye on my business. Even though my Lead Generation Company had gotten some great new business in the door, I was not there to carry out those deals or to make sure we were delivering our service. I was in bed and not paying attention to my business. We had a major financial reversal, and this ate away at my confidence and dropped me further into a depressive state. Just perfect, when added to self-loathing, physical pain, and depression. All the pieces were falling apart (coming together).

My dog Charlie, a fantastic and loving companion, was pulling me so hard on my unhealed, fused back during walks that I had no choice but to give her to my sister. I loved that dog and immediately missed her comfort. All dog owners understand how terrible it is to give a beloved dog away. Now I was completely isolated.

I was now in the worst place I had ever been in my life. A bankruptcy lawyer advised me to file for bankruptcy and said he would take care of it. He advised me that he would not go into his 401k to pay off clients who were demanding their money back. I seriously considered this, but even in that terrible state, I understood I could dig myself out by taking money out of my 401(k). My plan was to pay all the clients who had not received the service they paid for and to right the ship.

During this phase, like most clinically depressed people, I thought about ways to just end all of it. But when I thought about my kids and the message I would be leaving them with, I knew I could never do this. I thought about my natural fighting spirit, hidden, but still there. I knew I wouldn't do that, and I began to observe these thoughts, and I worried if I had created something I didn't want.

The problem, and this is a very serious problem, is that when you ideate ending your life and you have an emotionally charged thought, those thoughts that you begin to visualize... now you are creating.

My back started to get better. After about three or four more months, I decided I was going to be smarter in the gym and focus on my upper body. One day, while doing bench presses, I felt a shudder in my chest and heard a sound like a towel slowly being ripped. I had torn my pec major away from the tendon junction and torn the bicep. The tendon junction pec major tear is the worst pec injury, and in most cases, it is inoperable. To operate on a pec tear, it needs to be repaired back to the bone, but since mine was torn into the junction, my doctor told me there was no good operation for it, and it would probably never be strong again. It really is funny that I told my inauthentic self how smart I would be and just concentrate on my upper body, and now I've injured my chest, bicep, and shoulder as badly as my back.

So, my deconstruction plan was really gaining traction. I was newly divorced, depressed, hooked on hydrocodone, in constant pain from my back, chest, and shoulder, under financial pressure, and now came a cancer diagnosis. That's right. Remember, we talked about creating your life with thoughts, words, and imagination?

Here's the thing: I knew I had created cancer, and I'll discuss more on this later in the book. Once I realized it was me creating cancer, it wasn't a big step to figure out that I had created all of this, every single part of it. Why was it necessary to hit rock bottom? The answer is this: for some people on a spiritual path, it takes an enormous setback and a lot of pain to wake up. Shiva destroys to renew.

This life is not about perfection. I learned much more through mistakes, self-sabotage, setbacks, depression, impulsive behaviors, and other bad choices than through success.

As I mentioned earlier... when my good friend Tolo asked me when I would write and teach, my answer was, "Teach what? How to screw up my life?" His answer was, "Of course! You will relate to so many people. (I used a much more colorful word)

Tolo said, "Look at you, a contented man with much to teach." Now I understand what he meant.

One day, as I sat in my condo in self-loathing and back pain, I noticed I was urinating much more than normal. I had a bad feeling. I called my urologist, and he suggested getting a PSA test as soon as possible. The year before, my PSA had been 3.4. This rapid rise is called high velocity PSA, and it's not a good sign. He ordered an MRI, which showed possible cancer, and then a biopsy the week before my birthday. The results came back on my birthday: prostate cancer at 61. Happy birthday. Now we were truly getting to the rock bottom of things.

Let's recap: my business was in the dumpster, my body was wrecked from spine to legs and chest to shoulder, and I was alone, facing decisions about cancer treatment. My mind was in despair and isolation. I had been forced to give my beloved dog, Charlie, to my sister, and I had no real comfort in the world.

Suffering can be a trigger if you have the awareness that something more significant than suffering is happening. We learn so much more from our mistakes, thoughts, and actions if we just ask a simple question: "Why did I do this to myself?" Don't ask, "Why did this happen to me?" That will get you nowhere. The realization was that all of it, divorce, physical destruction, financial reversal, depression, and even the cancer, had a deeper purpose. I asked myself 1 important question: How is all of this to my advantage? The answer came back – Iron sharpens Iron. Out of the muck and mud, the Lotus Flower blooms. The Ibis Bird searches in the dark and brings forth sustenance.

I understood what I did and why - To wake up, I needed to see that I was not my body. I love my family, but my identity is not just my family, my body, or even my personality. In fact, I was disgusted with my personality, proneness to anger, and self-judgment and judgment of others.

Finally, I could take a deep, unattached look at this life and all the actions I've taken, both good and bad. I could begin to examine this life. You know the saying: "A life unexamined is not a life." The question is, how do you examine it? I was in no condition to meditate. I would findthe answer, and you probably know what my answer was.

The cancer is now in remission. My PSA is 0.015, which is considered undetectable after radiation. I am more content in my life than ever before. I find myself most often somewhere between contentment and bliss. I have had an awakening.

My interpretation of a Lao Tsu saying:

Thoughts become words

Words become actions

Actions become habits

Habits become character

Character becomes destiny.

My friend Tolo, as usual, was right. I am a teacher, I know that. It is my honor to write this book, and it is written first for 2 people. First, my 8-year-old self knew one day I would understand that there is more to this life. Second, to my 88- year-old self who will know, I hope, that I will continue to transform from the caterpillar to the butterfly. I never stopped. I knew it was my fingerprint. My path.

There is a saying, "Jack of trades, master of none." This saying was purposely shortened to change its original meaning and intent. It was originally, "Jack of all trades, master of none, is better thank master of one."

I have been guided and driven to learn because all paths lead to truth, in their highest vibration, and therefore there is value. It's has never been about rejecting. It's been about growing.

PART 2

DEEPENING THE SPIRITUAL JOURNEY

Chapter 3

The Initiations

As I lay down after drinking the cup of Ayahuasca, my thoughts began to take over. It's quite something to try to write about the most transformative experience of your life. Until that point, the most important moments of my life had been the births of my son and daughter, but what happened in July 2022 was beyond anything I could have imagined possible.

I thought this fifth ceremony might be my last time drinking Ayahuasca, and I hoped it would be special. My frequency and vibration had already shifted from previous ceremonies; I could feel it, and I knew it. The plan Mama Aya had devised for me in this experience was elaborate. As I lay down and the medicine began to take effect, I felt a tug at my hairline that ran down to my jaw on the left side of my face. Tingling followed, then a vibration between my eyes. I knew they were opening my third eye. I noticed my tongue and jaw had somehow shifted in my anatomy, and then an electrical charge seemed to run through me.

It happened so quickly and powerfully that it was like suddenly waking up and having to run full speed. As the medicine took hold, I heard an enormous, earth-shaking thunderclap followed by the sound of heavy rain. For a moment, I thought the storm was part of the Ayahuasca experience, but it was the weather outside the room, perfectly coinciding with the moment I felt my left side, near my hip, being "unzipped." A presence moved into my body, mind, and being. It was shocking and completely unexpected.

I immediately began speaking a language that seemed to come from me, yet was clearly of unknown origin, foreign, and ancient.

As I spoke, many unseen voices joined in, and I heard great laughter from the beings. It was like being thrown into a big, loud party suddenly without any warning. I was somewhere...but where? I realized I was speaking in tongues. So, this is what it is? Was it speaking through me, or was I only hearing it in my mind? Either way, we were together, and this was stunning. There are no words to do it justice.

The conversation in the tongue continued as "we "spoke to at least three or four other beings in that language. The communication was loud, lighthearted, and it was clear they were pleased I had joined them. It was the beginning of my direct interaction with other beings, a moment seared into my memory. He spoke through me to the others, and I could tell he was pleased by what he was experiencing, inhabiting my body, and I knew they knew my soul, my thoughts, and my heart.

Think of it like a software technician remotely taking over your computer, where you can see the mouse moving and clicking on your screen, only in this case, you are the laptop.

The night before, during the fourth ceremony, my hands and arms shook, vibrated, tingled, and moved nonstop for over two and a half hours. I also noticed that my forehead, both during that fourth ceremony and again the night before the fifth, had been vibrating and tingling for much of the evening. I feel strongly that the fourth ceremony, and the opening of my third eye, was preparation for this experience. This is why I mentioned earlier that there seems to be a plan woven into each and every Ayahuasca ceremony.

As I listened to the strange language and felt the high energy of their welcoming me into this awareness, I sensed we were no longer in the space where I had been. We were somewhere else, another location, another dimension entirely.

In the background, I heard the unmistakable sound of an otherworldly female giggle, mixed with male laughter. I had thought to myself, I think I have been here before.

Apparently, I had been there before, often enough that the idea of it being new to me was hilariously absurd to them. I had heard before that Mama Aya's giggle was distinctive, something you'd know instantly when you heard it. And I did. It was beautiful, ethereal, and joined the chorus of deep male voices. It was so incredibly....cool.

I found myself on the bridge of some kind of ship, or in an incredible world. I am not clear where I was. It felt like I was moving through space in the universe. I can't claim to know this with certainty; it was simply the feeling I had. When I think about the lightning, the powerful thunder, and the Norse myths of gods wielding such forces, I now understand it was their announcement that they were here. And they were here for me. I resisted the thought at first; it felt almost pompous. How could they be here for me? But I know now that's exactly what it was. The storm, thunder, lightning, and rain were happening in our physical third dimension, and it coincided precisely with the instant they took me over, moved me into their world, and I began speaking in their tongue.

I opened my eyes in the room with all the participants of the ceremony, to see how this medicine would work with my eyes – all 3 of them, open. Then I saw them, towering men, some with shoulders that must have been five or 6 feet across, and at least two to four feet taller than any normal human. They wore white robes and had powerful, commanding faces. It was clear these were supernatural beings, not of this earth. They walked past me slowly, staring directly at me as they passed.

Among them, I noticed a more average-sized man with an unusual, protruding bony nose and forehead, almost human, but not quite. His nose had a thick bony ridge running from the base down to the nostrils, giving it an odd shape. He looked at me with great interest, his gaze locking with mine. I knew instantly what he was thinking: So, this is your body now? His face was kind, and I felt an immediate sense of familiarity, as though we shared a friendship and that he was important to me. He stood there studying me, and as two enormous men approached and turned to face me, I realized: all of this was for me. That, and what came next.

As if this weren't enough déjà vu and supernatural strangeness, I later realized I had seen this normal-sized man before. I have owned, for many years, an Egyptian plate with his profile etched into it. I also possess a medallion bearing his face. Both belonged to my mother for at least thirty years, and somehow, I ended up with them after she passed away more than twenty years ago. I've included this picture of the plate of ancient Egyptian figures with similar unusual features, which appeared often in artwork over 3,500 years ago.

Some of the beings were walking around, and I could see their physical form, but the majority, particularly those speaking in tongues through me, were unseen. I realized that for me to go to this dimension and experience this part of existence with them, they needed to take over my body and, especially, fully open my third eye.

The beings were all around me. I heard their laughter and knew they were working in creation on some level, though I couldn't see exactly what they were doing. My observation is that they were using sound, vibration, music, and color to create a certain kind of reality that permeates the universe. They laughed as they created. I heard a lot of "ooohhhh" and "ahhhh," along with playfulness in this space as they bantered in their language when an especially interesting form was created. There was great joy, and I was enthralled to be in their presence.

I was encouraged to join and create with them. Meanwhile, I was flapping my arms nonstop in the room. Corrado, whom I became friends with after the ceremony, was observing me from two mats away for at least two and a half hours, listening to this strange language coming out of my mouth, as were others in the room. He said my arms were moving and shaking at a speed he could not comprehend.

At one point, two beings, shadow forms, came in and sat on either side of me on the mat. They were there to observe me; of that I have no doubt. I also knew they were protective. I could feel their need to observe gently. Their form was dark, with massive bodies, and it took me a bit to understand they were protective and probing my heart. The heart is the only thing that is of great importance in your acceptance into these realms of awareness. All the success, religious beliefs, practices, and meditation mean nothing without a heart centered and open. This quality has the most value of all.

My entire hands were moving at enormous speed, my elbows off the ground. I tried several times to stop the movement, but it was not possible. I was simply trying to see to what extent the movement of my hands and arms was important. They were determined to keep my arms and hands shaking and vibrating at incredible speed. As I said earlier, Corrado had watched me in fascination for hours and said he could not believe how long and fast I kept all this intense movement going. I now believe this movement has to do with wings, ascension, and transformation. And Dragons.

There were a dozen beings there, speaking together. They were still joyously laughing in their language, and even now I can hear their language and imitate it, although I don't know what the words are, but I do understand the feeling.

They were moving me to another state of awareness, another dimension or density. This place was beautiful, with strange structures and colors, gold everywhere, rich greens, and a frequency so unusual. I thought to myself, I think I've been here before. Then I heard laughter again from at least three or four of the beings. I knew immediately their thoughts: I then said, "Shambala," and they acknowledged my description. It was the most powerful déjà vu I have ever experienced. I have no doubt I have spent much time in this place.

I am writing this a full two years after the event, yet I can feel every bit of this experience.

My words are inadequate to describe the next event, which was the most mind-bending and powerful. It became very quiet, and suddenly I was alone. They left me somewhere in nothingness. Then I heard a crackling electricity. I could feel the electrical force, the buzzing, snapping sound of it. My mouth became very dry; my throat parched. I had absolutely no moisture in my mouth or throat and found myself unable to swallow. "Parched" does not fully describe this. I began to feel anxiety and thought, Not again. I honestly thought I might choke or suffocate.

Then my attention shifted to an even more intense sound, the cracking of something massive. Crack, crack, crack. It sounded like thick branches in a forest snapping in two, one after another. I then felt I was moved into a higher realm, and just being in this space was almost beyond my body's ability to exist. I knew this was HOLY GROUND. I was shaking and moaning. My hands were shaking uncontrollably, and I was moaning in this unknown tongue, and tears were streaming down my face.

It was obvious to me that I was in the presence of something beyond comprehension, something Holy. This was different. It was majestic. I felt strongly that I was in the Highest Dimension, the Highest itself...although how can we know what is the highest? It seemed, and felt, like a Throne of Holiness. I had said earlier that I had never experienced God in meditation or religious observance, but I can say with certainty: I was in the presence of something Majestically Holy. God.

To describe this with full disclosure: as I write this, I am experiencing kundalini, and my body is freezing with chills, confirmation of this explanation. I was in the presence of a HOLY BEING, FORCE, or PRESENCE that I could not see, but it didn't matter that IT was not visible. I felt it in my soul. I experienced this presence in my entire being. I wanted to prostrate myself before it as Muslims do when they pray, before the majesty of it. I have never had the inclination, feeling, desire, or need to do such a thing in my life.

I felt infinite love, infinite wisdom, infinite knowing of all existence, and infinite power bathing me. It is indescribable, although I will continue to try. I could understand how this QUALITY I was experiencing could imagine and create all existence. Of course it can!

I understood the word "infinity" and the word "knowing" truly for the first time. I had been initiated into the infinity of love in my first Ayahuasca ceremony, and now I was experiencing the power, knowing, and wisdom of all existence. I was breathing well now, in joy, bliss, and comfort I had never experienced before. I knew that the beings, Aya and Thoth, had orchestrated all of this. I had a powerful knowing of this. The creator speaks the universe into existence with reason and wisdom.

Everything is planned in the Imagination before its manifestation. It is the architect, the artist, the mathematician, the physicist, and the Creator who creates in bliss with a multitude of itself. The most powerful and stunning feeling was knowing how precious we are to it. The love I was given permeated my being so fully, warm and powerful in that light. I wanted to stay there and never leave. For the Creator, creating all existence and infinity, ALL, is simply within HIS knowing. It's as simple as that. It has always been here and always will be. I adore HIM/HER/IT.

This is quite a statement for someone who never truly understood the meaning of the word God or Creator or what prayer is, to say such a thing. As I write these words, knowing the truth of this, I understand the concept of gratefulness. And I learned, for the first time, what real prayer is. Prayer is not asking for anything; prayer is being grateful for what you have. And I am grateful beyond words or thoughts for the experience and the gift I was given. I was shown the meaning of love and wisdom, knowing and power. I did not want to leave. Ever. Let me stay forever, here. I was home.

Where is this? Where was I? I don't really know, but I do know it had HOLY POWER. It had a majestic, singular presence. It was elevated, this entire dimension, in the way that a throne would be elevated. I felt this was ITS home and its Majesty. IT HAD NO FACE, BODY, OR FORM. I was again covered in tears and had been whimpering for quite a long time. The facilitators at the ceremony were watching me and knew something extraordinary was going on, so they left me alone. They had heard me speaking in tongues, seen my arms moving for hours, and heard me moaning and whimpering.

At one point, Brandon, one of the facilitators, was speaking to me, his face a few feet from mine, but I could not hear a word he was saying. I was so deeply in medicine and this dimension. He was asking if I was okay. I lifted one thumb in the air, and he had a huge smile on his face and walked away.

Then, just as I found myself alone, suddenly I was joined by all the beings in this Most High, with the Holy One. I still don't know exactly who those beings were, the Elohim? Angels? I have no idea. But I do know they announced themselves with thunder and lightning, took over my body, and brought me to this dimension. My gratefulness has nolimit or proper words.

Another interesting thing I learned in my experiences is that music seems to affect them as well as the soul of a human being. The music that I heard was Holy. It had consciousness. The singing was conscious, not just the beings singing. We do more than just listen to music. It seems that in these higher dimensions, without a body, one can feel intensely on a level that the senses can never reach. Music, love, knowing, all these words have much more intensity here.

The teaching I was given is that creation is ongoing, and it is done with joy, laughter, powerful knowing, and reason. Existence was created in this joy, and it continues and will continue as the universes are expanded, held in place, and preserved. I was allowed to join them in this part of the experience.

I have not been the same since. They opened my third eye. When I close my eyes to sleep, I see purple and gold. I now channel my higher self, and many others.

How can everything that happens to you be to your advantage? Understanding this became the key to my life. I knew that everything in my life that had seemed devastating and beyond hope was, in fact, my own doing, and that I needed to wake myself up and find out what I could become.

Is it possible that life is as simple as this, to be the most authentic person you can possibly be and live this life with joy? Change is hard at first. It becomes messy, full of judgments, and difficult in the middle. But then I found beauty in everything. I realized you are always the onecreating everything, and that you have always been enough.

Chapter 4

The First Openings

(Part 2)

Ayahuasca is something you are called to do, although in truth, it's you who does the calling. Most people who have never studied Ayahuasca think it's just about hallucinating, so they dismiss it or dismiss you. They may lump it in with drugs like ecstasy or LSD. This is not to say that you can't have a life-changing experience on LSD-many did (the Beatles in the 1960s), but it's simply not the same thing.

Ayahuasca is a plant medicine found in the Amazon and in many other places beyond South America. It's a combination of the stems of the Banisteriopsis caapi vine and the leaves of Psychotria viridis, also known as chacruna, which contains DMT, N, N-dimethyltryptamine.

We all have DMT receptors, and several exist throughout the body. It's thought that one is in the brain or pineal gland and another in the stomach. Essentially, what happens during a ceremony is not just an experience, but a customized teaching through what shamans call Mama or Grandmother. I call her Aya, and I believe her to be God's emissary of nature on the earth (Gaia) and all evolving planets. I have heard her voice and seen her face, and I believe she is beyond time and space. Make no mistake, this is medicine, not a drug. Don't go to an Ayahuasca ceremony expecting a "good time." It is meant for serious seekers, for those genuinely interested in spiritual growth. You will learn what you need to learn. It is not about getting high. There are diet restrictions and pharmaceutical drug restrictions, including anti depressive drugs.

I have participated in over 20 ceremonies, and I can tell you this: I have never held a cup of ayahuasca in my hands without a flutter of the heart, wondering what awaits me. It's not always easy to navigate the space you enter. It takes courage to agree to examine yourself when you are truly looking at your real self. So don't let anyone, especially gurus or religious people with judgments, tell you what to expect and what to fear. There are many scientists who have done their own personal explorations of self through ayahuasca, who are better sources for the discerning mind. A recent study showed that PTSD sufferers improved morethan those prescribed the drugs in just one weekend retreat. The improvement lasted and outperformed every anti depressive it was compared to.

Those who have the most valuable Ayahuasca experiences surrender to the medicine. They know it is work and that it is serious. The surrender begins even before the weekend starts. For myself, I commit a week in advance that I will surrender, trust, not fight, and accept whatever I'm given. During the ceremony, remind yourself to be brave and to allow. This is what people mean by the phrase, " Spiritual Warrior."

As for purging, vomiting, or rushing to the bathroom, you are releasing something to receive the teaching. It's almost transactional in nature. No shortcuts. No deal-making. If you give this, you get that. Karma has a new meaning.

It is believed that Ayahuasca has been used for thousands of years in Peru, the Amazon, Costa Rica, and elsewhere. People in these regions often take small doses daily to kill bacteria, viruses, and disease, and many claim remarkable results. It cleanses you from the inside out, body and spirit.

For me, it was renewing. I felt it in my body and my brain, especially. I have, in my 60s, an equal recall of data and cognitive strength as far as learning and mastering new information as I did in my 30s. You may vibrate positively for days, even weeks, after your experience, physically, spiritually, and in your true self. I believe Ayahuasca was given to this planet to aid the evolution of humankind, and that the higher frequency you gain will elevate your spiritual self. With integration work and deep personal reflection, you discover, as I have, who and what you really are.

My brother John and I talked about the series Billions. I asked if he had seen the episode where Bobby and his brother go on an

Ayahuasca weekend. (Season 5, episode 1 and 2) He said yes, and almost at the same time, we both said, "Let's do it!" I probably watched three or four videos on Ayahuasca experiences, read everything I could find, and listened to several audiobooks written by Ayahuasca experiencers. I thought I was prepared... though you can never fully prepare for what you'll experience.

So off we went to Orlando a few weeks later. Before our conversation, I had no interest in Ayahuasca. But now, I felt called to it. If you had asked me then if I believed in God, I would have said I was open but doubtful, certainly not the God of books or organized religion, more like what Einstein called intelligent design. When asked if he believed in God, Einstein said he believed in the God of Spinoza, and he also remarked that God does not play dice.

We raised our kids Jewish. I was Bar Mitzvahed, and so were my children. Over time, I studied many traditions, three schools of Buddhism (Zen, Tibetan, and Nichiren), Hinduism, Kabbalah, Hermeticism, and, as discussed, Thoth and Hermes. I learned meditation over 20 years ago and even had some supernatural experiences through it. But to say I understood or had been in the presence of the Creator would not be true. I still, at this time, could not imagine God.

I went to explore with humility and an open mind. I let Aya know I would surrender to her as much as possible and that I was looking forward to her teaching.

I sat nervously with a cup of Ayahuasca by my feet. Within about 30 or 40 minutes, I started to notice the trees were somehow calling me. As I became truly aware of them, I noticed there were auras over the tops of each tree. I had never seen auras over trees before. The color of the aura was lighter than the leaves- a beautiful olive color, and in my view, lying on the mat, I could see six or seven large trees, each with an aura above it.

As I noticed the trees, I immediately felt and knew that they were living, breathing beings with souls. I had never thought of trees this way before, although when I built my first house, we built the driveway around a huge poplar. I admired that tree so much and did everything possible to save it. When I looked at these trees and acknowledged them for what they are, the trees began to acknowledge me. The crowns at the tops of the trees suddenly and gently moved forward toward me. There was no doubt, they were acknowledging me, and I was acknowledging them. I had this incredible feeling of connection between myself and these magnificent beings, and I received my first teaching: everything has soul and spirit, and sentience is not necessarily human in nature.

At first, I wondered, Is this really happening? Since I was brought up around medical doctors and consider myself grounded about what is real and unreal, I thought it couldn't be. But I was stunned by the reality of what I now know to be true, the power of these trees. I understood I was in another awareness, another dimension. It was more real than everyday life. The colors were vivid, and I felt the souls of the trees and my connection with everything around me. This went on, I would say, for 40 to 45 minutes, although there's no real sense of time in an ayahuasca experience. I had truly experienced nature like never before.

Then came what I'll call part two of the experience. I began thinking of all the people I love, my two children, my brother (who was going through so much and had so much hope for his own experience that night), and some relatives, particularly a cousin of mine. I noticed a kind of space opening, an orb of light, and then I felt myself slide into it, into this light. I asked myself, 'Is this the central sun of existence I've read about?' As soon as I asked, I dove deeper.

I thought about my kids, how much I love them, my parents who have passed, and all the important people in my life. I became overwhelmed with a sense of what love truly is. It was deep, all-encompassing, and so powerful in its intensity that I found my face covered in tears. This was not like the love we feel when we think about our families. That love is often filtered through the mind, analytically. This love felt different; it was the force that powers all existence. It's like nothing I can compare it to. When you're immersed in it, it's overwhelming. It's almost like exploding with love.

At one point, I thought, I cannot go any deeper than this. And then a voice, or thought, said: "Oh, you can go deeper." And I did. This went on for what felt like a long time. I dove further into love, into its power and its depth. I was in a soft, moaning, emotional state, beyond bliss. My shirt sleeve, where my face rested, was soaked with tears, so much so that I could have wrung it out like a sponge.

I had experienced the Heart of God. After this experience, I noticed on my right pinky a red heart embedded in the skin.

Once outside the constraints of the mind and body, in higher dimensions, the true force of love can express itself fully. It is stunning to consider that those existing in higher realms may experience this intensity of love eternally.

Part three of my first night of ayahuasca was an understanding of music, color, geometry, frequency, and vibration as the form of existence itself. As I became aware of the music being played, I began to experience it, not just hear it. It was almost in my DNA. The notes carried spirals, shapes, and geometric forms. I could see the music! Every note had a beautiful color. Every tone had a shape and vibrancy.

I understood that sound is of paramount importance. Light comes from sound, its frequency, its vibration, and fills the heart. Each note, each instrument, had a mathematical component, color, and shape. It became so clear to me how gifted we are with the ability to use sound to express thoughts. Every word we speak carries creative power.

So, this was my first ayahuasca experience. It lasted three and a half hours, and I was worn out in the most profound way. I considered all the years of meditation and reading and initiations and energy work, and this one weekend was 100 times more powerful than any of those methods of connecting I had ever experienced.

When I got home, I knew my frequency had shifted much higher than ever before. But I wasn't prepared for what came next. While walking Sophie (my dog), a bird flew straight at me, and within five feet of hitting my stomach, it veered off at the last second. Shocked, I followed it to a tree, where it chirped at me, staring directly. I asked, "What the hell are you doing?", but of course, no answer came. The sparrow just sat on the branch and stared at me. Sophie seemed just as unsettled as I was.

Later that day, still exhausted, I napped and vividly remembered my first 3D dream, which I now understand was a vision. A bat was slowly flying toward me, toward my consciousness, toward my head. Just as it was about to enter, I gasped and woke suddenly. I knew I was meant to remember every detail. Naturally, I googled "bats" to see what shamans say about them. It said it represented enlightenment.

At that time, I hadn't fully stepped into my power, so I was excited but unsure of what it all meant. A few days later, I was sleeping with Sophie curled on the bed beside me. Suddenly, I felt a tap on my right shoulder... then another… and then a firmer tap. I woke abruptly and looked at Sophie, thinking it must have been her. But she was sound asleep, paws nowhere near me.

I knew then I had been awakened by something else. Three taps on my shoulder. A message: You've been asleep. It's time to wake up. There's work to do.

Chapter 5

Clairvoyance

I sat outside with the Yawanawa Tribe, and 30 people were either in the medicine or, like me, in the afterglow of the ayahuasca-the DMT simmering the coals of the journeyed mind. I was the open-hearted man in that state, but after the ceremony, there is a bliss and satisfaction only those who have participated can understand. I listened to the singing, the bongos, and the flutes, and they were just gorgeous to the ears and soul. I learned many journeys ago that the Creator is literally responsible for every breath and beat of my heart, and the drums are special to Source because they are the metaphor for the beating heart.

The music continued to open my heart, and as is my custom, I wept in bliss and joy (Sat Chit Ananda) that such moments were now possible for me. My gratefulness and thankful openness were real, and it was gratitude from an open heart, with humility. These emotions, I now knew, crack open the cosmic egg and allow me to enter the inside, the Kingdom of God. DMT is called the God molecule for a reason!

As I walked to my tiny one-person cabin, complete with bed, table, lamp, and light, and sat on the bed, I again thanked the Creator, the cosmic beings, and all the others who took me to the highest lights of awareness. Again, this time my gratefulness was deeper, and with hands together under my chin, I was praying for the first time. I now understand that real prayer is giving thanks, not a laundry list of wants and desires. I simply said "I love you" to God, and I meant it from my very soul. I also thanked all of the others, Thoth, Aya, the Masters, the Angels, whose geometrical shapes are so enthralling, for their presence. I was in a state of gratitude that was overwhelming in its truthfulness.

At about 3 a.m., I was jolted awake. My eyes were still closed, but the visual field of normal darkness was different. It was inky black, and suddenly I saw, like white smoke against a blackboard in my mind, one letter at a time: I L O V E Y O U. As I write this, a cold rush of chills slides up my spine and goosebumps cover my body. They were communicating with me, or God was communicating with me, or both? My prayer had been heard. "You shall love the Lord your God with all your heart, all your soul, and all you might." The Shema had taken on the meaning it was intended. I had done that, and they (Him, Her, IT) had heard it.

The next night, I was still blown away by the previous night's communication, and I needed to tell them how honored I was that they would reach out to me in such a clear, powerful, stunning way. As I drifted off, I saw the black inky Mind Board and, in white smoky letters, one at a time, they wrote " IT WAS MY HONOR". I was even more stunned than the night before. How could it be their honor? It took me a few years to understand, but now I think I do. We are all precious to The Holy One, as a child is precious to a father or Grandmother.

This was made clear to me a dozen times, at least. We all love to watch our children grow and transform, and when we see progress or vast improvement, it's an honor to witness it unfold, to see the work put in and the fruits of it in our loved ones. It has been my honor, truly, to watch my incredible son and incredible daughter grow and transform. If I could, I would write it on their Mind Board, but constant calls and "I love you" will have to suffice. I had assumed after these two communications, they were over as far as contacting me, but it was just the beginning. After almost two years, it has expanded into fascinating and incredibly diverse communications.

Clairvoyance, by definition, is the ability to see beyond the range of ordinary perception. I believe it is the third eye that is seeing (or the pineal gland, once opened and connected to Source, that is doing the seeing). I distinctly remember on my fifth ceremony, before drinking the Ayahuasca, I had tingling and vibration in the center of my forehead, and I knew something was being prepared for me. Before the medicine had kicked in, I distinctly felt the tingling change to almost forcefully grabbing my forehead to my jaw and pulling that eye open.

Chapter 6

Manifestation

I have been studying manifestation processes, approaches, and techniques for 40 years. I have read more than 100 books on this subject alone. I put this knowledge into practice, at first with spotty results, which grew into a reliable proof-of- concept and, ultimately, stunning results that brought life- changing abundance. I will share examples from my life and outline my process.

I began my reading with the classics: Think and Grow Rich by Napoleon Hill (1932) and The Game of Life and How to Play It by Florence Shinn (1932). These two books are often cited as foundational texts in the field. Back then, they didn't use the word "manifestation." Instead, they explored the principles of thought, which ties back to the First Hermetic Principle, stating we live in a Mental Universe, a thought Universe. Desire and action must align, and these concepts converge in the more modern approach to manifestation. The power of thought and belief is paramount in shaping one's reality.

For those in business or creating wealth and abundance, there is another key ingredient: a well-considered plan of action. Napoleon Hill emphasized Definiteness of Purpose, focus, single-minded determination, and the ability to remain unwavering in the face of others' opinions.[7]

When I set out to create the businesses I founded, I always had a goal and a plan. I wrote down exactly what I intended to create: the monthly income, annual income, the number of people involved in delivering the product or service, everything. The marketing plan

7. Napoleon Hill, *Think and Grow Rich*, (The Ralston Society, 1937)

included not just financial goals but also my lifestyle. The idea was to improve my life and enjoy it as much as possible.

For example, my first company started to free me from selling life insurance. I was good at it, having just missed the Million Dollar Roundtable in my first year at Prudential, but at 23 years old, I disliked spending evenings in people's homes selling insurance. That was the norm in 1980. I started my first company to achieve two goals:

1. Work 9 to 5 in my own business.

2. Provide a much-needed service: in my case, I decided on a lead company...qualified leads for Property and Casualty agents.

Once my goals were clearly written down, I would speak them out loud with a firm voice and visualize, daydream about the new company. I was speaking it into existence. Many believe all of existence was spoken or sung into being. In that sense, writing the goals and plan was the first step, but intention and desire were what lit the match. Imagination dreams your life into experience, into the ether.

The last step, and perhaps the most important for me, was allowing it. Early in my entrepreneurial career, I often blocked my own success by letting limiting beliefs and fears creep in, weakening the creative process. It was a momentum brake on the magic. After my experiences with Ayahuasca, I could clearly see these limiting thoughts for what they were: the inauthentic me clinging to struggle. This pattern created loops of achievement followed by poor decisions, chaos, setbacks, and suffering. At times, I even expected setbacks, just so I could climb the mountain again. What a waste of time and creative energy.

At its highest condition, my mind is the Creator, directly connected to Source. I think of it this way: my little mind (you) is connected to the One Big Mind (God). I am a singularity of the multiplicity of All That Is, embodying all the power of creation for my own Universe, my life. I believe there are currently eight billion Universes on Earth, with, unfortunately, few people operating their own universe. This, I believe, is what the phrase "You are made in the image of God" actually means. We all have this power if only we would grasp it.

I started my first company at 27. I had the plan, the goals, a few clients, and even hired an astrologer to "birth the corporation" at the right time, giving it the best chance of success. We provided qualified leads by making direct marketing calls to businesses for liability insurance quotes. We set hundreds of appointments for our insurance agency clients. I quickly hired 10 tele-prospectors and a great manager, and we grew. I easily reached my written goal of $10,000 in income per month. Writing down my goals and speaking them aloud, while executing my plans, brought results.

Things were going well until I took on partners, who, as I later realized, wanted to own me as much as my company. By giving in to the limiting belief that they had something I lacked, I lost control of the company and the magic I had created. One day, one partner walked in and announced, "We're done with the company. We are out of business." I was stunned.

What I didn't understand then was that this setback was the best thing that could have happened. Failure is often the best teacher. My mantra, "Everything that happens to me is to my advantage", was not yet fully rooted, but the seeds were sprouting.

Here's what I did: I hired a good lawyer who negotiated a buyout of my partners. It cost me, but I regained ownership of my company. I bought used furniture at an auction, leased a cheaper office, found some receivables to fund operations, and rehired the 10 employees I had lost. I gave them two weeks off while I reprogrammed my mind for success.

During that time, I discovered Dr. Jonathan Parker's taped series on abundance and reprogramming the subconscious mind through affirmations. I had 25+ hours of tapes to study. So, I booked a flight to Tahiti, with nothing to distract me but those tapes. For 20 hours straight on the plane, I listened. Jonathan Parker's voice was so soothing and hypnotic that by the time I landed, I could feel the transformation. On the beach, I kept listening so intently that I burned myself to a crisp from not paying attention to the sun! I listened for another 15 hours on the flight back. By the time I landed in Baltimore, I was a creative force of will.

Eventually, I met Jonathan and studied with him for five years in Sedona and Ojai, California. His courses were very involved, and I was awarded certifications. I earned "Spiritual Healer," "Advanced Spiritual Healer," and "Intuitive Counselor."

When I arrived at the new office and all my employees were outside waiting to see the new office, I was like an unstoppable beam of light, and I had no doubt that we would do well. We took off like a rocket ship. I had learned to be the creator and never doubted myself or believed that others were necessary to create my outcomes. I learned that we are our own guru, our own teacher, and we have everything necessary inside of ourselves. This lesson served me very well in many other businesses.

The flow or current of creating must be nurtured, like adding a log to a fire, or it can be lost. I noticed that when I became distracted or caught up in negative people or thoughts, it affected my company. I later understood that my frequency was lower, denser, and more susceptible to negative thoughts. Abundance and manifestation, like money, are affected by frequency, vibration, and energy.

I continued to build my company, growing it to 115 people with 3 office locations. In business, you can run into issues of too much demand and not enough execution, and that's exactly what happened with Target Telemarketing. We had so much business that even outsourcing couldn't solve the problem. In fact, it hurt our reputation, because the quality of our outsourced company was just not good.

At one point, a client, a very large insurance company, said to me, "Jim, maybe we should just buy your company." The more seasoned businessman in me today would have said,

"Okay, let's discuss terms." Instead, inexplicably, I was non- reactive and allowed this opportunity to pass me by. I am currently a business broker, so the obvious line of thought would be: let's discuss valuation, terms, cash up front, and if there's a second, what's the interest rate and loan period? What would my employment situation be after the sale? So easy for me now, but the younger me, at 34, had no clue.

Here comes the lesson. It's all to my advantage, the good and the bad, but first, some background. While I had grown the lead company to 115 people, I was making less money each month due to the law of diminishing returns (constant overhead of hire/fire/train). At the same time, I started an insurance agency with a partner. We were an Impaired Risk Life and Disability agency, and the phone was ringing 100 times a day with agents needing our help.

I could have sold the lead company and grown the agency, but I was not clear in my thinking. There's a great old business conference speaker named Zig Ziglar (his real name), who called this kind of thinking' Stinkin' Thinkin'[8] with a southern drawl. I ended up selling the agency to my partner, and the telemarketing company died of natural causes. The lesson, since it's all to my advantage, is to let things go when they need to go. I didn't fully understand that opportunity had smiled on me: "Jim, maybe we will just buy your company." Jim should have asked about the terms!

In this life, we are both the cause (our actions, words, and thoughts) and the effect (what happens in our lives). I am responsible for what happens and how I respond or react to everything. After the dust had settled and I moved on from that company, I started to create in my mind another insurance agency. There are times when you just can't predict how a very small effort can produce very large results. This was one of those times.

I called one of the largest hospitals in Baltimore and asked the human resources director if I could quote their group life insurance. This wasn't a huge business, but I had experience in this type of coverage for large groups, and I thought it would be a good way to start the agency. The HR director told me there was no chance: "Jim, there's a good old boy network here, and you just can't get in."

By this time, I was 37, and I had begun to trust my intuition (most of the time). Two weeks later, on a hunch, I called her again. I said, "I don't usually call someone back after it's been made clear my services aren't needed, but it's like a birdie hopped on my shoulder and told me to call again." She laughed and said she was glad I

8. Zig Zigler, *See You at The Top*, (Pelican Publishing, 1975).

called back. Their union medical insurance had gone up 25%, and the carrier wasn't answering her calls. She asked if I knew anything about unions and medical insurance. Sometimes courage is better than brains, so I said yes and asked her to send me the census data for the coverage, and I'd see what I could do.

A few days later, 12 big boxes arrived at my office, filled with census data. I knew nothing about unions and almost nothing about health insurance, other than what I needed to get licensed. I had never sold a health policy before. I knew I could master the subject, but I needed a coach. I contacted an insurance continuing education teacher who taught health insurance, and he coached me just enough so I knew the right questions to ask and the right people to bring in.

I called the Union President, and we hit it off. I assured him I was on it and not to worry. Another lesson learned: always stay confident, read and learn as much as possible, and let the energy of that do the work.

I found a great insurance carrier that wanted the business badly, and both the manager and regional manager were eager for the meeting with the hospital's VP of Operations. They made their pitch, and I asked the key question: "These rates are great, but is there any way we can get the hospital a zero-deductible point-of-service plan?" (I had researched that this was the best possible plan.)

The Regional Manager of the Insurance Co looked at me, then at the sales rep, and then at the VP of Operations of the hospital, and said, "Sure, why not?"

That meeting resulted in my becoming their insurance broker. The hospital merged with six others, and I made more money on that one account than I had with all the companies I had previously started.

I had mentioned trusting my intuition, and my intuition told me I was on flimsy ground. I could feel it wasn't a stretch for them to decide they didn't need me, so I had already planned something else... a big, bold idea. I would go to Los Angeles and get a job as a talent agent.

I always loved movies. I had taken a few cinema courses to round out my pre-med curriculum and especially loved British cinema, especially David Lean movies. I used to watch movie after movie on Saturdays. My mother would drop me off at the Crest Movie Theater, and I would always watch at least two movies.

Within a week in LA, I met an entertainment attorney who decided to help me. She suggested I attend a black-tie event for Les Moonves, who was then the President and CEO of CBS Television. I met the right people at this event (I had definite purpose, desire, intention, and confidence). The next day, the William Morris Agency offered me a job as a talent agent.

At 40, I would be the oldest in the mailroom, but I knew the history and wasn't offended at all. I couldn't wait to start. In one week, I had landed the perfect job, I thought. It was at the very top of my list of manifestations so far.

My wife at the time was pregnant with my son, and we had built a large house, ironically, a California-style home, wide open with lots of stone and hardwood, but difficult to sell in Baltimore County. Then my wife was put on bed rest with our future son, so there was no way I could leave her and my daughter to move to California. I had to let go of that dream.

The William Morris Agency's HR director called me three times and finally said they never called anyone three times. They had planned on placing me with their top agent, and in two months, I would be an agent. "Are you taking the job or not?" she asked. I explained the situation, apologized, and that was that.

I devised another plan. I asked myself: What would be a pivot point at this time in my life? What alignment would challenge me at 40? I knew it had to deeply interest me, reflect my values, and give me a way to contribute and add value. I wanted to offer something completely different, to stretch myself. Not a service this time, but a product that could reflect my creativity.

Chapter 7

Permalean

I decided it would be a natural line of protein products, starting with protein powder that had clean ingredients and cool packaging. I hired a full-time graphic artist and his partner, who was also a talented illustrator and strong in copywriting. I found an excellent website developer, and things were taking shape.

It was 1998, and all of these ideas were fresh and new. I decided to call the company Permalean, as in "permanent leanness," and envisioned it as a lifestyle company, reflecting my own lifestyle. I funded the company with commissions from the health insurance business.

The first three protein powders were: Bodacious Berry, Chocoholic Chocolate, and Vigorously Vain Vanilla. Obviously, I planned to have fun with this company, and the product names reflected that. I named the protein bars Stark Raving Peanutz (chocolate peanut butter) and Moose and Squirrel (chocolate blueberry mousse). I quickly added a multivitamin (Nutricell), a metabolic tea with guarana, green tea, and caffeine (Activitea), and a metabolic capsule called Metaboost.

I partnered with a radio infomercial company, and we took off quickly. QVC had me on, and we did very well. Next, a Dr friend and I launched a one-hour radio talk show called Wellness for Life, which aired every week.

As I had anticipated, the hospital insurance agency account was terminated with a phone call. But in the very first 14 months of Permalean, we grossed over $1,000,000 in revenue, all in all, a very good result.

Lesson: Anticipate and prepare, listen to your intuitive voice, plan, write it out, and speak the creation into this world.

I enjoyed every part of the business, the talk show, the food brokers calling on retailers, the big orders from QVC, and later GNC. I ran Permalean for 10 years, and in 2007, I sold it. I had lost interest. I like to create, not manage, and I know this about myself.

The takeaway from all this business creation is that setbacks can always be handled. Nothing in business is smooth; it's like life on steroids. I always maintained a belief in myself and trusted that the right events would come my way. I trusted myself even when I made dumb mistakes. That trust and knowing are key ingredients in manifesting. Fear, anxiety, distrust, lies, and lack of integrity all lower frequency.

I always imagined the life I would live, the house I would build, and the material things I would enjoy. I wrote them down, spoke them aloud, and with executed plans, they happened over and over again.

PART 3

•

MYSTICAL AND COSMIC EXPLORATION

Jim Lowitz

Chapter 8

Mt. Shasta

I am on the plane to Mt. Shasta, California, as I write this chapter. I rented a house in Weed, Cal (interesting name), about 15 minutes from the tiny city of Mt. Shasta. I have the house for 5 days, so I can just hole myself up here and work, to get all of this down and communicate in words. I started this book 4 years ago and thought I had writer's block. It was delayed so that I could write about these experiences and then record them all, like a good reporter would do. I have had experiences that are clearly designed to share. It's a very strong "yes" to tell all of this. Now, when I start writing, it is sometimes joyful for me to reread these experiences.

I had prepared to sleep, and with my eyes closed, I noticed my Mind Board was not black. It was now purple-violet, or pink-purple in color. It has been almost 2 years now since the color changed. Sometimes I see orange and green, but it always starts with violet colors, then that color fills the entire visual field of the Mind Board/ Eye. I later learned that many people see purple colors with their eyes closed, and it is understood to be the Third Eye opened.

I was jolted awake, and I saw this: "Jimmy, This is You! "… and then an arrow sweeping across to the left, pointing at a man sitting in a chair with his back to me, a pen in his hand, and this: "When will you start writing again?" So, after a month or more of procrastination, I started to write again. I certainly felt encouraged.

They also strongly suggested I end a poor relationship with a woman I was seeing, with this: "Sever ties with …." I must admit, I did not comply as quickly as I should have. They were, of course, completely right; she was draining my power and distracting me from growing. I was surprised by this because it was new, and it was a directive. I contacted my friend Tolo, a true psychic medium for Spirit, and I asked him, "Do they tell you what to do?" He just laughed and said, "They sure do." In a way, I was relieved to hear Tolo be so whimsical about the whole thing.

As I lay in bed and drifted off to sleep, I was awakened by the hooting of an owl. It seemed to be in the bedroom; it was so loud. It was a series of three hoots, and that reminded me of the three taps on my right shoulder, long before the clairvoyance began, and after my first Ayahuasca experience. I had been home for a few days, asleep on my left side, when I was suddenly awakened with three taps, the third one particularly firm. I immediately looked at my dog, Sophie, and she was fast asleep. So, it wasn't her, and I doubted she could firmly tap me on the shoulder. I immediately knew it must be them, whoever they were. This was all very new back then. I got out of bed and in an even tone I said, "Uh, can you please not do that again? It scared the shit out of me."

Getting back to the three hoots, they made it clear then and now that they were watching me. In fact, they sent me a video of an owl that slowly blinks its eyes, and they even wrote (to dumb it down for me if I didn't understand the metaphor), "We are watching."

I have heard my name loudly in the room, "Jim!", sometimes in a strong male voice, sometimes in a female voice.

I had been studying the concept of being the Universe, all existence, and experiencing Sat-Chit-Ananda. I had been initiated into Kriya Yoga. As I was walking Sophie around the lake in Lakewood Ranch, FL, where I live, I needed to pause because I could not feel my body. Then, I didn't know who I was. I couldn't remember my name or what I was. I was at the lake, then I was the tree, then the gravel road. I looked at Sophie and thought, maybe I am Sophie, or the birds. I stood completely still in this awareness, and suddenly I was everything, and not me. It lasted maybe 20 seconds, because as soon as my inauthentic mind/ego chimed in with its inadequate, finite, judging brain to explain what was happening, it ended. That was quite a moment. There is so much that is planned in this life beyond our comprehension, and maybe it's not meant to be comprehended. There is a great saying: once the seeker has stopped asking questions, they have found it.

As I shut my eyes and drifted off, sleeping deeply, I heard a beautiful female voice singing. I awoke to her voice first in the dream, "Free your Tree of life", and then her voice filled my bedroom again, and finally a louder third time: "Free your Tree of life." It was so otherworldly, beautiful, and clear. I moved to lie on my left side and was guided to take a deep breath. As I inhaled and then exhaled, the Universe came out of my mouth, and I merged into the Universe.

As I type these words, I feel two things:

The familiar chill and goosebumps when I speak the truth.

I understand. Four years ago, I certainly would not have believed it either. I promise you this: I am not allowed to lie or be out of integrity in any way. This has been made clear to me. Our bodies are a metaphor for the Universe, with the vibrational frequency chakras, but we also contain the Universe in our being, literally, and I was shown this, and I am reporting this. By breathing out the Flower of Life and then the Universe, and becoming it, I remembered who and what I am, and what all of us are.

We all have the Universe within our souls. The awakening is the memory of who and what we are. I am that I am. I am that I am and what I will be. I am that I am and what We Can Be. You are life, and life is life. Kabbalah teaches that the body dies, but life is always life. You never die. Life cannot ever die. Your body dies, yes, but not the authentic you. The authentic you is everything, the All.

Chapter 9

The Dragon from the Sun

I wear a Feng Shui Pixiu bracelet. It originally came in copper, but it quickly tarnished, so I melted down an old gaudy gold bracelet and made a beautiful gold mold of it. The beads are inscribed with the Mani chant, and I added a few other meaningful charms. The Pixiu is a two-headed creature in Chinese mythology. It has the head of a dragon and the head of a lion, and it is said to offer protection, abundance, good fortune, and prosperity. It symbolizes balance, power, and the need to harmonize opposing forces. I certainly do not disagree.

I have to say, I love this bracelet. And when you wear a dragon bracelet, sometimes you forget, but your dragon does not forget, apparently.

I began seeing dragons in January of 2024, and later I learned that 2024 was the Year of the Dragon. I have included in the photos in the book some of the sky spirit cloud dragons that appeared to me many days throughout 2024. I showed my friends Tim and Jenn the pictures, and they, too, routinely saw them in the sky. In some of the photos, you can clearly see bones protruding from their heads, their teeth, long tails, and wings. One picture even looks like an X-ray of a dragon; it's that clear.

I also included the dragon that appeared in a Hindu vessel, a diya. As I lit the oil lamp and began meditating, I was guided to stop and look at the brass cup. The tiny half-inch flame shot up at least four inches and kept shifting into different forms. I quickly captured it all on video with my phone. There is one image where the dragon appears so clearly, sitting comfortably in the cup, as if posing for a picture. That photo is in the book.

There is also a Yod (backwards), the first Hebrew letter of the name of God, as well as an alien head, all distinctly formed in the flame.

Sometimes, the entire sky was filled with dragons, and I've included those pictures too. I always compliment them for their beauty and their presence, and they continue to visit me.

As I lie in bed and begin to close my eyes, not even in an alpha state, I see my violet and pink Mind Wall, and there before me is a dragon, clearly happy to see me. I look at him (or her?) and say telepathically, "Look how beautiful you are!" The dragon rolled on its back, wagging its tail in glee like a loving dog welcoming its owner. Things were changing with my communications with dragons.

Across the street from my Florida condo, I love to watch the sunrise over a huge lake that flows into the Manatee River. I bring Sophie with me, along with my rocker chair, to really enjoy sun-gazing, a practice I've been doing for more than five years.

The practice of gazing at the rising sun dates back millennia and spans many cultures and religions. From Egyptians worshipping Ra to Greeks honoring Helios, the sun has long been associated with divine power. Native American and Indigenous cultures hold sunrise ceremonies to greet the new day and recognize the Creator's presence. In Hinduism, the rising sun is an auspicious time for spiritual practice. In Buddhism, it represents an opportunity for enlightenment. Christianity holds Easter sunrise services symbolizing resurrection, while Judaism considers sunrise the renewal of creation, both physically and spiritually.

One morning, Sophie and I sat together as the sun peeked above the buildings across the lake. I watched its familiar pulsating colors, deep green at the center, with pink and violet hues radiating around it, moving in spiral patterns of power. A pink path stretched across the lake, filling it with sparkling light. Then something new happened: I saw geometric shapes in the sky, followed by an Om symbol. Suddenly, blue orbs burst out of the sun and drifted toward me. I saw the sky painted as if in brush strokes, beautiful shapes. It was as if a great painter had decided to demonstrate just how easily it could create beauty that I could enjoy observing.

At least ten or twenty blue circular orbs surrounded Sophie and me. She watched the birds behind us, while I was transfixed on the orbs. Then I looked up and saw an enormous pinkish-red dragon flying straight toward me.

Yes, I know it sounds unbelievable, but it happened.

The dragon skimmed low over the lake. Its magnificent face was clear as day, at least ten feet wide. I could see huge vertical bones protruding from its head, and I could clearly see its eyes, mouth, and teeth. Its body stretched one-third the width of the lake, making it at least a hundred and fifty feet long. Sophie and I were frozen, our eyes following it in stunned silence.

The dragon circled around us and returned, allowing me one more impossible, breathtaking look. It looked directly at me, almost as curious about me as I was about it.

I hesitated to tell anyone about this experience, not even my Ayahuasca tribe friends or others I know who are open to supernatural events. I had one friend I could and did speak to. He had experienced dragons. I asked him if he felt this was a spirit animal for me. His answer was succinct and short: “It’s your dragon.”

I took my son to Kauai a few years ago for my birthday week. I had rented a beautiful house with magnificent mountains to the left and a clear view of the ocean. We had a great time, nonstop. He had been clear about the week: “Dad, I don’t want to sit around.” So, we did just about every tour I could find.

One day, we took a two-man all-terrain vehicle trail, flying around the mountains all day with so much dirt on us that it took two days of showers to get it out of our skin and hair.

So much fun!

My cousin had suggested that I take lots of pictures because she felt something supernatural was going to happen, and to send her all of them, which I did. I took beautiful photos of the ocean, mountains, sunsets, sunrises, you name it. Kauai is so special. There are so many legends about it, ancient gods, spirits, brave warriors, the Menehune, love stories, and so much more.

For me, it’s the topography: the cliffs, the waterfalls, the sheer power of the place. The energy is palpable to anyone who visits. Only God could create such beauty, the greatest artist, architect, and designer.

One day, as I was leaving the house in the car, I was guided to take a picture at the stop sign at the end of the road. The photo was average at best, a nice mountainous green overlook. I sent my cousin a few dozen pictures, and she called me: "Take a look at this one and enlarge the upper left corner!"

I've included in the book both the original photo and the enlarged section. In the deep, cloudless blue sky sit two sky beings, just them, nothing else around.

The thing that blew my mind is that the faces of the sky spirit beings had the same unusual features as the man/being who stared at me (as if he knew me well) during the ceremony. They had unusually pointed chins and wide-set eyes, exactly like his. He had communicated to me telepathically that he knew me well, and I knew then that in another long-ago life (or parallel life) we had been good friends. His face was unforgettable; he could not have walked around Mt. Shasta, Sedona, or Baltimore without being noticed.

I have also included a picture of an Egyptian plate my mother gave me (yet again, Mom gifting me a stone on my path). The plate depicts a king, Thoth, perhaps, sitting in a royal chair. At the bottom of the chair legs are carvings of two male beings. Their faces and pointed chins match those of the sky beings. I am convinced these are the same two beings, and that one of them visited me more than three years ago during my second Ayahuasca ceremony.

This has been the theme of my life now: walking in both the physical matter world and the other real world. These same two sky spirit beings also appeared to me in Florida, right in front of me in the sky. They stayed there for at least 30 minutes.

From the Kauai house to my left, there were massive mountains where I could see 6 or 7 enormous faces carved into the rock, side by side. Each face was 75–90 feet long, some broader, some slimmer, some with hats shaped like those of Sumerian gods. Some looked directly at the house; others were in profile. They were clearly defined and mesmerizing. I looked at them every day and kept taking pictures, but because I was too close to the mountain (I think that was the issue), the faces never showed clearly in the photos.

A month later, while sitting on my lanai porch couch, dark clouds formed before me. Out of them appeared one massive face after another, seven in total, each very distinct, staring in my direction. (I get chills as I type this in confirmation of its truth.)

I have to say that two or three of the faces were fierce and intimidating, so much so that I could barely keep my gaze fixed on them without turning to a kinder face. The feeling was unmistakable: I was in the presence of Royalty, of Cosmic gods.

Here's just a small sample of the dragons in the sky that I constantly see. If you look I am sure you will find them too.

I was guided to open my eyes while meditating. The usual single 1/2 inch flame lighting the cup shot up several inches as if alive and morphed into many forms, settling as the dragon you see gently sitting as a cup of fire. It remained there while I photographed and videoed it. This was the beginning of seeing dragons and it's continued for years.

Chapter 10

Aliens, Cosmic Beings, and Remote Viewing

I am writing this portion of the book in Mt. Shasta, and I am feeling the amazing energy. It's my 5th day here, and I love the house and the views of the mountain. I've included pictures of the house and the view.

As I drift off to sleep, I begin to feel the familiar vibration, trembling, and shaking of my left hand, almost like Parkinson's, I would imagine. The Mind Board turns to clouds of violet, filling my entire visual field. I see an unusual alien, one I have never heard described. Its head is shaped like the gray alien that everyone knows about, but it's quite something to see. One side of its face is pink, and the other side is white. It stares directly at me. Did it visit me, or did I visit it?

The next night, I am awakened, and the usual process unfolds. This time, I see the two-colored face alien standing next to a normal-looking man who is sitting by a small desk. They are talking to each other. Then they both turn to face me. I have clearly interrupted their conversation. What happened here, I wonder? Is this some kind of inter-dimensional or parallel-world remote viewing? I have never read about this. They stare at me for a moment, clearly, they see me, and then simply return to their conversation, as if it's no big deal.

A few nights later, I vibrate awake, eyes still closed, third eye wide open. The purple-violet clouds form on my Mind Board, dancing until the entire field is filled. I see four Anunnaki men standing together, the same beings many have seen depicted in Sumerian tablets and Babylonian art They are faced away from me, and I can see their large wing of brown, white, and golden colors, reaching slightly past their knees.

As I look at them, one turns toward me and stares directly at me. The other three continue their conversation and don't turn around. The one watching me has a magnificent dark braided beard and a broad, striking face, not one you'd ever see on this Earth. He seems amused that I am "photobomb visiting." I say, "Good to see you!" and he turns back, just as the alien and the man had done the night before. Clearly, I have again interrupted someone, something I'm told I do often in ordinary conversations. I suppose not much changes, even when traveling in dimensions of awareness. My good friend Tolo once said to me during a reading with Spirit: "Wow, you can go anywhere." I am sure this is what he meant.

About a month passed, and I began receiving almost daily written communications from a variety of beings. One group told me they were my Spirit Guides, and they provided their names. Others did not.

Unfortunately, most of the time, I can't read the writing. It's too fast, and it's not in white smoky letters. (I believe the white is reserved for the Highest, since I've only seen it a handful of times.) Most often, the writing is in darker colors against the purple background, moving too quickly for me to follow. They sometimes put a flashing light at the beginning of a letter or sentence to help me focus, and when that works, I can read it. I realized recently that some of this content may be intended for my higher self to download, not for me to consciously read.

Often, several groups are writing at the same time, filling the Mind Board with dozens of lines of commentary, impossible for me to fully comprehend.

The next night, immediately after closing my eyes, the purple Mind Board reveals an alien face, again, unlike anything I've seen before. From the side, its profile is unusual, with a nose at least four inches long. I saw 2 eyes. Then, as the full face comes into view, I realize it has five eyes (3 eyes on the other side of its face) and two more noses. Two faces in one head with two eyes and a nose, the other side with three eyes and a nose. Like the pink-and- white alien, it is divided into halves.

I accept this as a visit and a gift and admire the Creator's extraordinary work. Then I wonder if he looks at me and thinks my face is strange, so simple and limited in form and function. Wouldn't five eyes and two noses come in handy? I let the thought go and drift into sleep.

The next day, while sitting on the porch with Sophie, I am guided to look at the sky. Dark gray shapes form, and I know how to watch carefully. There, I see two beings with the exact same five-eyed, two-nosed, double face. They are looking directly at me. I waved to them and thanked them for visiting.

This is quite something, the contacts I'm having in the higher frequencies of the third-eye Mind Board are also consistently appearing here in this third-dimensional Earth reality.

2 Beings Of Light: My cousin Eileen encouraged me to "take lots of pictures - something unusual is going to happen in Kauai." I stopped at a stop sign and took this pic. She noticed the 2 beings of light in a perfect blue sky. I saw them again in front of my condo in Florida.

PART 4

PERSONAL TRANSFORMATION AND SELF-REALIZATION

Jim Lowitz

Chapter 11

Parallel Self - I Meet Me

I drift off to sleep and am awakened with my left hand throbbing, shaking, and vibrating. I see a face I've seen before, it's mine. I know it because, even though he's lying down (as I must do to connect), I can clearly see the mole on the left cheek. The face is unmistakably me, looking so young... age 35, I would guess. This time, he's lying next to a beautiful woman with green eyes, and she's also looking at me. *(Any chance I can meet her in this world this weekend??)*

Suddenly, I somehow moved toward him and hugged him (me). I can feel his thick curly hair. I had those thick ringlets back in my college days. I had forgotten how full my hair was then, and, sadly, it is not now. I'm stunned at the quickness and impulsiveness of my action, and I know I startled him. I just had a powerful need to hug him/ me and communicate. I suspect we are not supposed to touch our parallel selves, and I have not seen that me since.

Chapter 12

Celebration: The Cycle Is Complete

The date is 7/7/25, which adds to 21, which reduces to 3. This number is one of synchronicity, creativity, and self- expression. It encourages sharing with the world, embracing one's individuality, and welcoming personal and spiritual growth. It's also a number of new opportunities and dreaming big. When repeated many times, it's a powerful message from the spiritual world, a sign of Divine support, asking one to listen closely to intuition.

Tesla said, *"If you want to understand the Universe, think in terms of 3, 6, and 9."*

As I've grown into this state of awareness, I understand that, in essence, that is what we are: Awareness itself. We are composed of just this one thing: God. That's it.

It is no longer possible for me not to notice the repeating numbers, the whispers, the pats on the shoulder, the "coincidences" that are so much more than coincidences. There is bliss in the noticing, *sat-chit-ananda. "You shall love the Lord your God with all your heart and all your soul and all your might."*

I drift off again, and my left hand vibrates and shakes. The familiar purple clouds fill my Mind Board, but then pink, orange, and green flood the landscape. Fireworks are going off, and so many beings are writing on the board. I can't read it all, as usual, but I see winged beings and many others, thumbs up everywhere, it's just like a party going on. It's a celebration! They are writing: *"Way to go, Jimmy!!"*

I have completed the cycle. I'm not sure which cycle this is, but, alright, alright, alright.

I have completed one inch of a million miles of track.

Jim Lowitz

PART 5

ANCIENT WISDOM AND UNIVERSAL TRUTHS

Chapter 13

Thoth the Thrice Great

Thoth is a very special subject for me. Before reading and studying The Kybalion[9] and The Emerald Tablets[10], I had not synthesized what I had learned in a way that could be integrated into my daily practice. It was through these texts that I realized Thoth was my teacher. Through his words, I could expand my consciousness and grow.

Thoth is known by many names. He is called Tehuti and Hermes, as the Greeks believed Hermes to be the reincarnation of Thoth. He is often referred to as Thrice Great, the greatest king, the greatest priest, and the greatest philosopher. Thoth is said to have built the pyramids and to have ruled in Khem from 50,000 BC to 15,000 BC. In those ancient times, the land was called Khem, not Egypt, and the wider world was Atlantis.

There are examples of these incredible lifespans in many tablets discovered, but the summary of long-lived individuals is famously described in The Sumerian Kings List. Eight kings reigned over 241,200 years according to this tablet, but many are normal periods of time. I.e., 10-20 years. Thoths' long life does not seem so impossible when considering the Kings List and other artifacts describing these long lives.

He is typically depicted with the head of an ibis and the body of a man, holding a writing tablet in one hand and a stylus in the other.

9. The Three Initiates, *The Kybalion- A study of the Hermetic Philosophy of Ancient Egypt and Greece Authors,* (The Yogi Publication,1908).
10. Maurice Doreal, *The Emerald Tablets of Thoth the Atlantean,*(Independently published, 2022).

The very words chemistry and alchemy originate from Khem, just as the word thought derives from the name Thoth.

Thoth was known as the builder of the pyramids and the teacher of writing, geometry, astronomy, mathematics, astrology, magic, medicine, philosophy, and architecture. While most often shown as a man with the head of an ibis, he is sometimes portrayed as a baboon. The ibis' head itself carries layered meaning: the curved beak resembles a crescent moon, often depicted with the moon above its head. Symbolically, the ibis also places its head into the dark mud to find nourishment, a metaphor like the Buddhist teaching of the Lotus Sutra, striving through the difficulties of life to transform.

It is said that Thoth wrote more than 30,000 books. I would have to say that he is my teacher. I wear an amulet of Thoth around my neck, showing him with his ibis head and his hand holding a pen and a writing tablet. It is also said that when the Library of Alexandria was burned to the ground, the writings of Thoth were lost forever. The Kybalion, also known as The Kybalion by The Three Initiates, and The Emerald Tablets are channeled writings of Thoth. Whether or not the material in these two books was truly channeled, the information and ideas are undeniably powerful.

What's interesting is that, as I mentioned, my mother gave me my grandfather's Masonic ring when I was 21 years old. I was intrigued and then fascinated by what I had learned about Masonry from the books that were available. I felt I could come to know the character of my grandfather, who had died when I was 12 years old, by becoming a Mason, but even more importantly, I wanted to learn.

At that time, I didn't fully grasp the connection between Thoth and Masonry, but I sensed there was a strong possibility. If initiations had originated in the pyramids and their purpose was spiritual evolution, then the parallels within Masonry seemed convincing. The idea that the fingerprints of the Degrees of Masonry might have originated with Thoth became increasingly compelling to me as I continued to study. There is integrity in Thoth, and that integrity is central to becoming and then living as a Mason. There are many false conspiracy theories about Masonry. There are people who may have corrupted the true message of Masonry, but I assure you that the tenets are powerful, and the goal is to build character with integrity and truth.

Writings about Thoth often call him a god. Thoth himself claimed that he renewed himself in the pyramids and traveled to Amenti 100 times. Amenti was said to be found under the pyramids through a portal of some kind.

Clearly, if he lived and ruled for thousands of years, he was no ordinary human. It is said that he descended from the Blue Race, the Arcturians, though he was still human. The teachings of Thoth are called Hermetics, named for Hermes. Thoth's names are many, but his most well-known is Thoth/Hermes Trismegistus, the Thrice Great. It is believed that Hermes was the reincarnation of Thoth, as was Quetzalcoatl and others.

Thoth said, "Three are the powers given to the masters: Infinite Wisdom, Infinite Love, and Infinite Power."

The Seven Hermetic Principals:

1. All Is Mind. Everything Is Mental.

Our senses know that the infinite, living mind of THE ALL is the law. We are part of THE ALL. The universe is the creation of the mind of THE ALL. The universe is mental.

2. The Law of Correspondence

As above, so below. As below, so above. What you do in the mental plane affects the physical plane. What you do in the physical plane affects the mental and spiritual planes. Every thought has a corresponding effect. Everything influences everything else. All planes of existence are connected and affected. Through the principle of correspondence, you bring manifestation from the higher planes into your life.

3. Nothing Rests. Everything Moves. Everything Vibrates.

Spirit is one end of the pole of vibration. It may appear still, but it moves so rapidly that it is beyond the physical. The highest level of vibration is spirit. The other end of the pole is slow vibration, denser matter. As you raise your vibration or frequency, your spiritual connection to THE ALL increases.

4. Everything Has Poles

Everything has its pair of opposites, identical in nature but different in degree. Hot and cold differ only in degree, not in concept. Up and down are the same concept, just on different poles. Energy and spirit are the polar opposites of matter, energy and spirit being the high end, while matter is the low, dense end.

All vibrations are essentially the same, but matter is so dense that it appears solid. It is our perception, our senses, that limit us. We do not perceive energy and spirit directly, only matter.

We can move from anger to love because they are not absolute opposites but different vibrations. Fear can shift into courage, and hate can transform into love, because they are the same in nature, just on opposite poles.

5. Everything Has Its Ebb and Flow

Everything has its rhythm and seasons. All things rise and fall, come and go. Like the swing of a pendulum, rhythm manifests in everything. It is "good timing." Some people always seem in rhythm, always at good timing. The principle of rhythm is key to contentment in life. There is a time for action and a time for rest and reflection. Stay calm, understand the principle, and avoid panic. Work with the rhythm of life, not against it. You are the cause, not the effect.

6. Every Cause Has Its Effect. Every Effect Has Its Cause.

Everything happens according to law. Chance is merely a name for a law not yet recognized. There are many planes of causation, but nothing escapes the law. To create your own universe, you must understand that chance does not exist.

If you notice an effect, its cause may lie in the spiritual plane. Create new causes in your life. The outer world is the effect of the causes you created in thought and word. There is no chance, only vibration, energy, and frequency taking form as matter. Choose your vibration.

7. Gender Is in Everything

Everything has masculine and feminine principles. Gender manifests on all planes. The word gender comes from the Latin meaning "to beget, to procreate, to generate, to produce."

Masculine and feminine are the Yin and the Yang. Masculine is connected to will. Feminine works with thought, concept, and imagination. Without feminine energy, the masculine acts without restraint, reason, or order, leading to chaos. Without masculine energy, the feminine becomes stagnant and complacent.

When these two energies, will and imagination, combine with careful action, they bring forth manifestation. Masculine and feminine must be balanced within yourself for creation to occur.

Thoth is such an integral part of science, consciousness, and the understanding of universal order that it is impossible to overstate his importance and relevance. Everything seems to point back to him.

Pythagoras went to Egypt to study geometry and mathematics, spending more than 20 years there before returning to Greece. The Greeks revered the ancient Egyptians (not to be confused with modern Egyptians). It is not a stretch to assume that in Egypt, he was learning principles first developed in the land of Khem and passed down to the Pharaohs.

There also appears to be a relationship between Thoth, Kabbalah, Abraham, Moses, and Enoch, as well as connections with Quetzalcoatl in South America and the pyramids found there.

There are dozens of enormous pyramids around the world. According to Graham Hancock and many archaeologists, these pyramids share unmistakably similar architecture and knowledge.[11] Many are even larger and older than those in Egypt, debunking the idea that the Egyptians built them all.

---

11. Graham Hancock, *Fingerprints of the Gods: The Evidence of Earth's lost Civilization*, (Crown Publishing, 1995).

As Thoth himself said: "Builded I the pyramids." It is time to give the greatest architect that ever lived his due.

More On Thoth's Own Words from The Emerald Tablet.

"I think the beyond, beyond life and death, is formless. Master of all that exists. Free of time and space.

I am a being of earth and fire. Be thou only fire. (He is saying: be your highest self, your soul.)

Ask THE HOLY ONE to flash a ray of light, a shard of His illumination.

The soul is permeated by mind, and mind is permeated with ATUM (God).

Gods are immortal men, and man is a mortal god.

Mind is the divine part of man, emanating from the mind of ATUM.

The soul is nourished by air and fire, the body by earth and water.

Mind is nourished by light alone.

Speech is an image of the mind, and mind is an image of THE HOLY ONE. (This is how you are in the image of God, through your mind as it connects to THE ONE MIND.)

The body returns to nature, the spirit to the cosmos, and the mind to ATUM.

Everything is made of the Holy One. Nothing is composed of anything else. This oneness unites everything.

The divine light is the mind of God.

The nature of God and His mind is to create. The nature of man's mind is to think.

Show me the nature of reality. Bless me with the knowledge of ATUM.

ATUM is one. When divided or multiplied, He is still one. ATUM is everywhere and everything. All is ATUM. His mind is how He contains the universe and the cosmos."

"Ask to receive a shard of His illumination into your awareness, so that you may know the sublime mind of creation.

Hermes saw time as a circle, a year being how long it takes the Earth to travel around the Sun.

The Sun is the image of God, nurturing and feeding energy to the planets so that nature may sustain life.

The physical cosmos is the result of the mind of the cosmos. ATUM created the cosmic mind, which creates the cosmos, which creates time, and time creates change.

The essence of the cosmic mind is permanence.

The essence of the cosmos is beautiful order.

The essence of time is movement.

The essence of movement is change.

The essence of change is life.

The cosmic mind is ATUM.

The cosmos dwells in eternity.

Time dwells within the cosmos.

Change dwells within time.

Man was created to behold the beauty around him from God.

To know the nature of reality, LET ME KNOW the mind and thoughts of ATUM."

"Like the number one, all numbers are derived from it; everything comes from the One.

Light and life are experienced as thoughts and feelings.

Mind gives birth to speech.

The desire to know God is enough to set you upon the path of enlightenment.

The human mind is in the image of the One Mind.

God is present in the material world around us and in the immaterial thoughts within the mind.

THE ALL and THE ONE are identical, and like the number one, cannot be multiplied or divided.

All is many things, many selves, yet still THE ONE.

It is the many subsumed by the One, ATUM...the oneness that embraces the parts.

All things are thoughts that the Creator thinks. All things are Mind. This is how He contains the universe.

If you cannot see thoughts, how can you expect to see God?

The Word was the coming forth of the dark waters of chaos into light and life, into mind and soul.

The cosmos, the universe, is the whole nourishing its infinite parts. It was created through the thoughts of the Holy One. In His mind is the Son of ATUM.

The soul is permeated by the mind.

Energy flows into eternity. Everything moves by the power of the soul.

The soul is illuminated by the mind, and the mind by God. The soul fills the body of the cosmos and gives life to it."

"God created the world so that we might see Him and know Him. He is here, looking around. Everything is made of Him. Nothing exists that is not Him.

Humble amazement is the prerequisite to knowing Him.

Mind is known through thought, just as God is known through creation. God is not invisible. He is everywhere for you to see. Look.

Since He is always creating, this is His very nature, we can always see Him.

The number ten is unity. It de rives from one; therefore, it is holy.

God is not only one mind, He is the cause of the One Mind."

Chapter 14

Kabbalah

The Kabbalah originated as an inner esoteric teaching of Judaism. It is a method of teaching passed from master to disciple and from teacher to pupil. Kabbalah is the Hebrew word meaning "to receive inner wisdom from mouth to ear." This is an oral tradition. There is no single book called Kabbalah; it is a body of knowledge.

There are two primary texts: The Sepher Yetzirah (The Book of Formation)[12] and The Zohar (The Book of Splendor).[13] There are various spellings of the word Kabbalah, reflecting different historical periods and traditions. It can be transliterated as Kabbalah or Kabala (Jewish tradition), Cabala (Renaissance Christian tradition), or Qabalah (Western Hermetic tradition).

The term Tree of Life was popularized during the Middle Ages. The ten Sephiroth (emanations or spheres) within each circle, or Sephirah, represent vessels of energy. Energies across from one another balance each other: mercy without severity is weakness; severity without mercy is cruelty. The Tree of Life is a visual representation of the path of return to God. It can be used as a template for a multitude of systems, offering understanding and allowing one to arrange life in an orderly way, like a filing cabinet.

The Hebrew word for hand is Yod. The fingers of the hand have 14 bones, and the numerical value of 14 corresponds to the word Yod.

12. Akiba ben Joseph, *Sefer Yetzirah: The Book of Formation, (Martino Fine Books, 2019).*

13. Gershom Scholem, *Zohar: The Book of Splendor: Basic Readings from the Kabbalah,* (Schocken, 1995).

This is a glimpse into the genius and beauty of Kabbalah: letters connected to values, to numbers, to sound.

The Merkaba is the name in Kabbalah for entering the mystical realms. Mer means spirit, Ka means light, and Ba means body; together, they form the 'chariot of God.' Merkaba is the fifth-dimensional garment that connects you to future perfection. It is a spinning field around the body, depicted as four wheels.

Fire is the radiation of energy. Water is the absorption of energy. Air is the intermediary, the spirit.

Ein Soph is the eternal state of all things. All things arise from Ein Soph, it is the cosmic egg. From it emerges a central point and an abyss. Ein Soph produced the primitive air, or abyss, like a chaotic sea. Man's body is enveloped in the causal body, or auric egg, of man, the supreme consciousness of God. When I experienced Bufo, I felt as if I had cracked open this cosmic egg. When I heard the cracking sound before being escorted to the Sanctuary of Eternity, I also felt that my shell of material reality was also being cracked.

Ein Soph is divided into three parts: Ein (pure spirit), the limitless spirit, and limitless light. From Ein Soph comes The Supreme One. The supreme individualization of Ein Soph is the Holy One, One Mind.

The infinite created a single point: the first emanation, the first crown.

The earliest opinion is that Abraham wrote The Sepher Yetzirah.

The 32 paths (Lev Dalet) spell "heart." The path of the universe goes through the heart to the mind and the cosmos.

God is both nothing and the Infinite All. Zeros and ones. It is the void, it is one, it is zero, and it is the All, Ein Soph, the Infinite, Living, Eternal Mind. There are now many scientists and physicists who believe our entire universe is composed of zeros and ones. It is so fascinating to me that science and Kabbalah seem to be in agreement.

Kabbalah is extremely complicated to study. It is more akin to studying science. I'm not qualified to oversimplify Kabbalah, because it cannot be simplified. Therefore, I've simply highlighted a few points that have fascinated me and held my interest.

Part 6

INTEGRATION

Chapter 15

Integration

I turned to spiritual traditions not for answers or theories or ancient beliefs. I turned to them because something within me was already speaking -- a calling. My Life experiences and my studies took on an interconnectedness.

At first the different traditions and teachings I studied felt like a new pair of glasses that clarified something and gave new language to a part of what I encountered in everyday life.

Kabbalah spoke in letters and emanations as though Creation itself were articulated, explaining itself. Hinduism spoke of consciousness "playing at being many" incomprehensibly long cycles of time. Buddhism spoke of emptiness and compassion as being inseparable.

Hermeticism spoke of correspondence "as above, so below," as if reality was reflecting and mirroring itself in every possible measurement.

What Vedanta call Brahman, manifesting as Maya, Hermeticism calls vibration - nothing static, everything in motion, it appears solid because of our limited perception of light and sound of this body we inhabit.

For me there is more clarity found in Hermeticism, and it feels like the link to all other traditions. Like the ingredients in the perfect onion soup tasting reality. In Hindu tradition of Vedanta, this depth is called Brahman -- the absolute reality, beyond form, the source from which all appearances arise and which they return. The cause of all things. The Upanishads say simply: 'Tat Tuam Asi - "That Thou Art."

KABBALAH	VEDANTA
• Ein sof "without end"	• Brahman-The Absolute
• Beyond name, form, thought	• Beyond name, form, thought (ninguna)
• Prior to god as known	• Prior to gods as known
• Source of the Sefirot	• Source of all manifestation (Maya)
• Cannot be grasped, only lived	• Cannot be grasped, only realized

For me, Vedanta as "only realized" has deep personal meaning. Both traditions insist on the same paradox: The absolute is unknowable, yet more intimate than the self.

As I further turned toward Buddhism, there was no eternal substance, no Brahman, no absolute self, no ein sof. Instead, I encounter Sunyata - emptiness. It is not emptiness as despair. It is emptiness as freedom. It is the emptiness as the absence of anything held or owned or possessed. This includes the self that I once believed myself to be.

At first these seemed to me to be incompatible. One or more traditions speak of the absolute. Another tradition refuses it. One names being. Another rejects every name.

Brahman is not a "thing."

Ein sof is not a "being."

Emptiness is not "nothing."

As I sat with all of this: The infinite of Kabbalah, the absolute of Vedanta, the emptiness of Buddhism, again the link to all of them through Hermeticism shines through for me.

Reality did not depend on belief, culture, or a god language. It doesn't begin with worship - it begins with certain specific laws. Reality is an ordered living intelligence governed by 7 principals rather than commandments or guidelines. I believe that Spinoza, Einstein and Tesla would find Hermeticism immensely interesting.

It is not faith or obedience but understanding and clarity. Thoth seems to say "read this - try it on for size."

Understanding, for me, did not arrive through just study or just plant medicine or just through divine communications. It combines with all these things when patterns reveal themselves and are recognized. I found consistency through the orderliness when I looked for it. Its the same profound intelligence moving through Hindu cosmology, Buddhism in all its forms of negation, Hermetic principle and Kaballistic wisdom.

There were important wake up calls for me. They may have had different expressions or symbols or languages but Sat Chit Ananda flowed through all of them: Existence, Consciousness, Being and Bliss. The bliss through which EXISTENCE waits.

The being behind the face was never a figure speaking to me. It was my authentic self, waiting patiently for me to recognize my true self, and finding that which was forgotten.

Chapter 16

The Play of the Human Being

Alan Watts was one of my favorite authors on Zen Buddhism. He had hilarious and powerful teachings on the "path of no path," as written by the British-accented mystic. He moved the needle for me. He stirred the pot and opened my inquisitive mind. But it took many years to truly understand and then experience his teachings. What did it mean that we are an aperture through which the Universe (God) knows itself? How could we be the author of our own life and be the main character, the actor, the writer, the producer, and even the director of our own life? He said, "You created it, so stop complaining about it and figure it out! Own it." I understand now what Alan Watts meant, and The Play of the Human Being took on a meaning I could never have imagined.[14]

As I sat for my most recent ceremony of Ayahuasca, I asked again to know God. I asked for the courage to surrender to the medicine and to allow anything and everything. I promised to purge without hesitation.

I knew my body was clear as a channel. I had stopped eating meat several years ago and rarely drank alcohol or took drugs or medications. I felt unusually prepared. I stated my agreement to be in humility and be a spiritual warrior. I agreed to be and was open-hearted. I spoke to my inauthentic self and made it clear: "You are not invited into this sacred place tonight."

---

14. Alan Watts, *The Book: On the Taboo Against Knowing Who You Are* (Vintage 2011).

My practice each morning is consistent and ingrained. I surround myself with meaningful items. I begin, sometimes at 3 a.m. or a little later, but always before sunrise. I start by lighting three lamps with organic oil, which are spread around my living room, illuminating the space. I then burn incense, usually sweet frankincense, to add my favorite fragrance. I choose my favorite hape, which puts me in a grounded and expanded connection. Then, I meditate with Kriya yoga meditation techniques. I often listen to frequency music and Om at 432 Hz. I take monatomic gold under the tongue, which increases my connection to higher frequencies. I finish this portion of my morning process with a cup of ceremonial cacao. The feeling of contentment after the cacao is just wonderful.

Most mornings, I watch the sunrise with Sophie, my shnoodle companion, and off we go to the dog park. At some point, I sit on a bench and recite many different prayers and chants. I honor the deeper truths that are in my lineage, as well as truths I have learned in my studies of all the religions. They intertwine in my experiences and shape all that I am now.

I start with the Shema (Jesus' favorite prayer) and say it in Hebrew, and then the 23rd Psalm of David. I recite The Mani chant (The Dalai Lama's favorite chant), other Buddhist chants, and Hindu chants, including Om Namah Shivaya and a few words written by Rumi. I recite myfavorite poem from the *Book of the Dead*, and I add what I am feeling in that particular moment. There are times when I feel pulled into older, ancient times during these few minutes of prayers, and it is Holy Time to me.

I watch the violet colors coming off the sun. Sometimes I see blue orbs flying out of the sun. I have seen the symbol for Om written in the sky in front of me several times, along with other symbols that I don't recognize.

As I waited for the cup of Uni (Ayahuasca), I asked to receive a profound experience. I don't usually ask for this, and I knew from prior experience that I was really "asking for it," and I better buckle up. When I have asked for this particular transcendence, it comes with stunning clarity and intensity.

The medicine begins to kick in and grabs hold of my mind and body. My head and jaw have that familiar connection. It's always a bit of a shock because I can feel this world fading and the real world coming. The geometrical being, or is it an Angel, is moving toward me, and I see all its complexity, its colors, varied shapes, and lines. I even see, for the first time, its face. I never knew it had a face! It notices me noticing it, and I know it is pleased. I complement it, and I am grateful that this night, I am calm enough to be aware of all the details and can let this being know I see its beauty. (I believe that the first beings were the first forms, the Platonic solids, and the first Platonic solid was the tetrahedron.) This being resembles the geometric shape of the tetrahedron.

I am moved to a larger, more expansive, higher-density dimension. There are Archangels, Cosmic Beings, and Ascended Masters. I believe there are Spirit Guides there, too. There are just so many of them, and I feel their powerful presence of light and knowing. There are no bodies here to see, but the Power, Love, and Wisdom are stronger than anything I could conceive of. It's a celebration of some kind. As I am moved forward, I suddenly realize: It's for me! For me? Why? What have I done to earn this? I certainly am quite clear about the mistakes I have made. Very clear. I immediately feel unworthy of this attention. In my life, I have certainly not been pure. In business and in relationships, especially in my younger years, I was prone to exaggeration, lying, manipulation, rudeness, smugness, stupidity, and pompousness. I had to show people my success. "Look at my house! Look at my car! I am this and I am that." I was like a preening peacock with muscles, screaming, "Look at me!" It's a hole that stuff can never fill.

As they ushered me into yet a higher awareness, I felt again the presence of a Holy Throne. I remember clearly my fifth ceremony when I was in this higher presence of what I can only describe as Pure Love and Light. I stood there shaking, trembling. I glanced at my left hand, and it was shaking and trembling, like the rest of my body. As I stood there before this group of beings, I said, "NO, NO! I AM NOT WORTHY OF THIS ATTENTION. I AM NOT. THIS MUST BE A MISTAKE. IT'S NOT ME. IT CAN'T BE ME." A voice enveloped my head and said, "This is exactly why it is you, and why you are worthy."

I was moved away from the "Throne," and I began to watch real human lives, what I can only describe as The Play of the Human Being, simple lives, moments of farming, families, and interactions that seemed mundane to me. Scene after scene of just life. It was people just living their lives with the usual ups and downs. Life, death, and mourning. Birth and then inevitable aging, suffering, joy, sadness, pain, and more of the same.

The beings, including the Most Holy, were all watching The Play in this sacred place, and they seemed riveted, enthralled by the experiences. They were moved by the everyday struggles of human existence. They seemed to be saying to me that human life, in all its ordinariness, was something of unimaginable value. Perhaps these were my lives or possibly the lives of others. It didn't matter. What mattered was the way they watched, with full presence and awe. We are so precious to them. I felt it, and it was overwhelming. Their love and devotion to all of us is real. It is real. I felt infinite affection. I felt the Creator's love and pride. I am moved as I write these words and remember this experience vividly. They are all so involved in our lives. Dozens of them for all of us as we create our lives. There are 8 billion people, 8 billion universes created on this planet by creators who don't even know they are doing the creating. We are always with our spirit guides, angels, and other beings. We are never alone. The play is always watched.

As I returned to the Sanctuary of Eternity, I had agreed to accept the honor that was granted to me. It felt like I was being welcomed home and had completed something ancient. A cycle was completed, and it was worthy of great celebration. There was a feeling of a crowning. This moment had meaning...of exactly what, I don't know.

Then something happened. I was lying down and began to feel droplets of moisture of some kind on my face and head. Drop, drop, drop, drop. I quickly opened my eyes, expecting that someone was spraying me with water in the ceremony as part of the ritual, but no one was near me. Everyone was just in their private experiences, so I closed my eyes and immediately felt the drops again and let it happen. Is this what the mystics call anointing? I am not claiming a thing. I am reporting to you exactly what happened. I know this for sure. I am not permitted to exaggerate, lie, or embellish anything in this book. They made this very clear to me.

And then the letters came.

With my eyes closed, I saw a radiant color of purple, as I so often see when Spirit communicates. But this time, the space was filled with Hebrew letters and words. They were rolling very quickly. I had the feeling these words were being downloaded into my soul. They were flowing, streaming, and pouring through me. They were glowing. I don't read Hebrew very well. I recognized them instinctively, Holy Script, familiar and foreign all at the same time. The words were somehow from within. In Kabbalah, it is said that Hebrew is the language of Creation, the first language. Each letter has a vibration and frequency. Each letter has consciousness.

As I was watching the Hebrew letters filling my very being, and the drops continued, I listened to the tribe singing and chanting. It's not in English. They don't speak English. In fact, they need a translator into English for the leader to be understood when he talks to those in the circle who are drinking ayahuasca. As I listened to the beautiful chanting with drums and flutes, I heard the unmistakable word Torah. It can't be. It must be part of the dimension I am visiting. He was clearly repeating the word Torah, Torah, Torah, Torah. I was coming out of the medicine. I had been very, very deep, and now I was out and feeling, well, divine. Pun definitely intended. Now I heard a word very similar to Adonai, repeated over and over, and then more Torah.

I wanted to speak to the leader through the interpreter after the ceremony ended. I would have to wait for daybreak, when the ceremony ended. The three of us stood huddled together. I told the interpreter about the experience I had. He considered each word, and I asked him, "What did the word Torah mean in his language He looked at me and said, "It means God." I was stunned. How could a small tribe that has been in Brazil for thousands of years and requires a long boat ride through the waters, followed by a trek into the forest to find them, know the word Torah and know it means God? They simplified Torah, which Jews believe was inspired by or directly from God.

I walked outside to be alone and try to integrate what felt to me like years. The Play of the Human Being and the preciousness that we are all held by the Most High, and all that happened, so much detail, so vivid, moving, and powerful. I was glowing like a beam of light. This was unlike anything I had experienced (and that's saying a lot).

Okay, there's a celebration for me, and a crowning achievement is recognized. There are drops that could be some kind of anointing, and then, while the drops are hitting my forehead and face, I see the word Judah, and it relates to me somehow. Then a tribe from the Amazon, with no relationship that I have ever heard of with Hebrew or Judaism, is chanting Torah over and over again. They understand Torah to mean God, which is stunning. The synchronicity of all this happening at the same time, the same moment, is mind-numbing, inexplicable, and gorgeous. The perfect metaphor for the unknowable and the awe of Source, The Great Spirit, The Holy One, Unity. Oneness is synchronicity. There is no time. It is a concept to separate events in the dream world of the Play of the Human Being.

A Tapestry of Letters and Crowns

In that special space where time and space dissolve, I found myself sitting at the intersect of worlds. The Hebrew letters appeared before me, radiant and Alive, as if purified in light. Each letter was more than a symbol; it was a living frequency, a vibration of the divine. I felt their consciousness. They flowed and rolled before my eyes, and I understood that these letters were the Blueprint of Creation Itself and contained the Names of God.

The Kabbalists had long said that in the beginning, though there was no true beginning—the letters of the Hebrew Alphabet emerged from the infinite, forming the language through which the Divine spoke the Universe into Being. To witness them was for me to see the very code of Reality, the architecture underlying all things.

Chapter 17

The Dissolving, I Am Awareness

The Bufo Toad secretes a potent hallucinogen, 5-MeO- DMT. They say it is five times the strength of ayahuasca.

I have experienced more than 20 journeys with Ayahuasca and thought it inconceivable that anything could exist five times the strength of Ayahuasca. I can confidently say I was wrong in my belief, which is why beliefs are so undependable when measured against experience. I met the facilitator of the Bufo, and like all of my experiences, there is a ceremony built around the medicine that becomes intertwined with appreciation and gratitude. There are specific guidelines observed during and before the ceremony of smoking the toad. An example of these guidelines is that the facilitator sits directly behind you, and there is to be no speaking or touching during the experience.

I have always marveled at the courage required to participate in any of these entheogenic substances. There has never been a time that I did not give respect and reverence for the power of these medicines. There has never been a time that I was not nervous as I stood to receive the cup of ayahuasca or was preparing to smoke the toad for the first time. It is a test of courage and a symbol of my commitment to grow, transform, and become without fear or judgment. The courage is in the surrendering. This, again, is the meaning of the term Spiritual Warrior.

I knew that most people who smoked the toad collapsed backward, their bodies surrendered to something far greater than themselves. But that's not what happened to me. Not then. Not ever. Each time I inhaled the sacred medicine, I remained upright, anchored somehow. My hands extended out before me, palms down, almost instinctively. It was as if my body already knew this posture. It was some kind of remembrance. It was a mudra, I found out much later.

As I held in the inhale, something opened instantly, and I was taken. No time to orient myself, no gradual easing in. I was flung into a realm or dimension or frequency, pure geometry, pure light. I was surrounded by octagonal shapes and forms, like honeycombs made of gold, luminous and breathing with divine white light. They were not just shapes; they were living. These geometrical shapes vibrated and pulsated, and I had melded into the shapes.

An intelligence moved through their lines, as if the architecture of the cosmos had momentarily shown itself to me. I knew that I was in the center of The Mind of God. The force of power, knowing, wisdom, and love was with me, of me. The drop of the ocean is the ocean.

And then, I don't know if I went inside the octahedron or if it came inside of me, but I passed through some threshold, and that's when it began.

I screamed. Not metaphorically. I screamed with every fiber of my being, in a way that I have never screamed in my life. A primal scream. Not from fear, but from the sheer force of what was happening. My ego, my identity, my personality, my stories, my history ripped away. Torn from me like a husk of corn. And beneath it all, there I was. Not the "me" who writes these words. Not even the one who witnesses his own thoughts. Deeper than that. More ancient. More real.

I was being stripped down to the core of my soul. I could feel it, raw, real, and infinite. After the screaming came the language.

That language/ tongue that has emerged in my Ayahuasca ceremony three years before, and then so many times later.

It was flowing out of me. A language I have never studied or ever heard spoken, yet it comes through with such power. Sometimes it feels like a language I knew before this life. Before the speech. Before I thought.

The tongues poured from me as I entered a kaleidoscope space, a mirror-drenched universe of light and color, a living spinning mosaic. It was as if creation itself was spinning around me. The colors were alive, just as I knew colors were alive from my first medicine experience. They were sparkling, flashing, and multidimensional. The speed of it was incomprehensible. How could you not scream? I wasn't watching it. I was in it. I was it. I was in the engine room of reality, caught in the act of becoming.

I heard myself saying: "Oh my God. I am God." Not in arrogance. Not in delusion. Not in ego. It was the opposite. What remained was the stillness behind all things. It seems to me to be the divine having a moment of remembering itself through me.

The sacred "I" behind the "I."

And then there it was. A light in the upper left corner of my vision. A star, small at first. And as I looked at it, I watched the entire universe being sucked into the star. Condensed. All of it, every moment, atom, every sun, every galaxy, is being gathered into this one blazing point of light. Was this the Omega Point?

A vertical line cut through the star, and then a horizontal one. And then the star blinked out. It disappeared. And there was nothing. No light. No geometry. No color. No form. It was inky blackness.

Just me. Just awareness. And in that moment, I knew, not as thought, but as a fundamental truth, I knew what I was. I was aware. I was aware. The universe was gone, and I was alone in this nothingness, but I was aware that I was still here! I am that I am. I am aware. I was aware, but I was my truth now. I was nothing, but I was still something in my awareness. Yes, I was alone, and as I came out of this experience (which lasted 15 or 20 minutes), I was smiling. I was in bliss. Was this Samadhi? Was it Nirvana? Maybe. Either way, I'm fairly sure it's about an inch in those million miles of track.

I didn't really know what to call this chapter. "I am God" might frighten or even outrage some. But for me, it's not a claim. It's a confession. A remembering. Waking up is remembering what we are, if we go deep enough.

Robert Adams said, "As you follow the 'I' to the heart, and the atoms, and the sub-atomic particles, going deeper, going back, back to the source, to the energy waves, to the void, and finally your entire body is totally dissolved and consciousness stands alone."[15]

15. Robert Adams, *The Silence of the Heart*, (Acorn Press 1999).

Chapter 18

Marked By The Heart

It was my second weekend ceremony in medicine, and I walked over to a table filled with the most delicious hummus, carrots, and cauliflower you can imagine. (Food after ayahuasca is on another level when it comes to munchies.)

I began to notice something I could no longer ignore. On the upper left side of my right pinky, near the nail, was the red shape of a perfect heart. It was deep red, raised, and unmistakable. There was no pain at all. A dermatologist might explain it, but it sealed itself like a sigil.

I am a Gemini, ruled by Mercury, the planet of communication. The pinky finger is Mercury's domain. And now the message I am meant to carry has quite literally formed itself into my finger.

Love.

That is the message. And now I wear it, sealed on my skin.

Chapter 19

Thoughts And Insights

The purpose of the ego is to allow you to maintain the illusion of separation and to promote forgetting that you are an immortal, trans-dimensional being from a much higher awareness. This reptilian brain, as discussed earlier, offers no wisdom, but it does provide vital protection and survival instincts. Without it, you would not be able to negotiate this existence. The ego comes from the Infinite. It does its part, which is to convince you of this dual nature, or maya. It is vital to have the ego; otherwise, the game of transformation could not happen. You would be unity, and there goes the game. This game of transformation is not easy. As President John F Kennedy said, "We go to the moon not because it's easy, but because it's hard."[16]

The soul is not in the body so much as it created the body. The body is housed in the soul, and the body navigates the soul. You are the water navigating within the body of a celestial ocean.

Everything in this game of existence, and it is a game, is resistance. As Lao Tzu said, "Be like water... nonresistant." Conflict is a game of consciousness, and to win it, you must be okay with all of it. Everything that happens is to your advantage. It really is. The creator is in water because nothing in existence can survive without it. Water reacts to frequency and vibration, and it responds to thoughts. Dr Masaru Emoto found that water exposed to positive loving words formed beautiful, symmetrical shapes and crystals, while water exposed to negative words and emotions formed asymmetrical, distorted shapes.[17] Essential for life, water is treated in a sacred way by Hindus.

16. JFK, Spoken at Rice University, Houston, Texas, (September 12,1962)

17. Dr Masaru Emoto, *Messages from Water*,)Hado Publishing,1999)

They have special containers for water, placed in special areas within the home.

I personally keep my water moving by putting it in a glass vessel that constantly creates a vortex. (There is a product I purchased that creates this spinning vortex in the water.) I can't explain in scientific terms what I receive from this "living water," but I love watching that vortex swirl, greeting me in my condo and inviting me to take a sip. All of my friends and family agree that this moving water tastes thicker and velvety. In earlier times, we drank from moving streams, cold and perfect. Now, we use plastic pipes, adding chlorine and other poisons to our water supply, stagnating this life-giving element. If God is in the water, that is not a good way to treat the Great Spirit.

The brain, or ego, will keep you in conflict. That is its job, along with making you believe this is all real, that this ego construct can save you, and that you need saving. You're not aware of the game. Waking up means you become aware of the Game, and then you make the rules.

Doubt, fear, worry, and anxiety are nothing more than a cloud of thought that has no permanence. The cloud soon fades away, and to observe it without reacting seems to me the most difficult aspect of this life. It is certainly my challenge. Once you have an awakening, your thoughts, words, and actions are always at the forefront of your being. There is no going back from awakening. Integrity becomes paramount. To be dishonest, to cheat, steal, lie, or exaggerate with manipulative intent is simply not allowed. I've noticed that it seems to be a law: if we give you this, then you get that. As my friend Tolo said, and as I'll say again, there is no going back.

Watch your words. They contain creative energy. Every thought that carries an emotional charge, whether love, hate, anger, fear, jealousy, or laughter, becomes like a battery once coupled with deep emotion.

Add emotion to a word, and the secret to creating your world is revealed. I am. I create. You are creating this life with one thought, word, and action at a time. You are the cause, and your thoughts and words are the effect of your life.

Manifestation = current = currency. Current means "occurring in or existing at the present time." In physics, current is the rate at which electrons flow past a point in a complete electrical circuit. This existence is electromagnetic in nature. To be "in the flow", another definition of current, you must be present and connected. To manifest what you want in a linear future, you must believe and experience what you want right now, even if it does not yet exist in the present moment.

This is why manifestation experts understand that they must first imagine and emotionally experience what they desire. Then they create the circumstances to have it in the eternal now. There really is no future and no past. If there was a past, go back to it and tell me what you find. If there is a future, please tell me what it is now. I'd be fascinated to know. But there is only this now. The past and the future are folded into this one infinite moment. The concept of Eternity is now. There is always now. If I ask you if it is now, you will say yes. We can continue this conversation for eternity because it is Always Now.

When further considering "currency" and "current," it became clear that the word currency means energy, and that money, called currency, is also a form of energy.

When I first started studying manifestation in my early 20s, I would carefully write down what I wanted. I wrote down exactly what I wanted in my bank account, what my lifestyle would look like, and who the right woman would be.

As I developed this system of manifestation, it became quite clear that as I leaned into thought and imagined myself living a certain life or attaining a certain goal, these goals became reality. Making myself believe this new reality was the engine that drove the machine, my created life, my manifested life. The magic, for me, was flowing in the current.

I saw it repeatedly. I would read my business ledger books from 10, 15, even 20 years ago and see how I had manifested what I wrote down by first imagining it happening. But I had to include a vital aspect of creation: I must plan and execute my goals. Simply wanting something, or saying "I want this to happen," only kept me in the state of wanting.

I now only state what I want to experience as my new reality. For example, I made $1 million in 2025. Then I imagine myself experiencing what that feels like, and then I experience it. I feel the wish fulfilled. That's the secret. I never say, "I want," because all that produces is the endless wanting of whatever it is.

I enjoy the process of writing it down. I love sitting with a notepad and a pen and writing my life. You are truly the author of your life, and you play all the parts. Once you're certain about what you want, and you begin executing the plan you know has Already Happened, the universe conspires and structures reality in ways you could never anticipate or imagine.

This is why many manifestation experts say, "I never imagined I could have this." I'm currently buying insurance agencies for a client, and we are in this together right now. He recently said to me that three years ago, he never imagined this life. I told him, "That's because you and I are now in the current, and your positive manifestation, multiplied by mine, and this power is creating in ways neither of us could have foreseen."

In 2017, when I started to hit rock bottom (and didn't fully get there until 2020), I had forgotten my manifestation capabilities. I had forgotten that in a depressed state, I was manifesting limiting, painful, and fearful experiences through my thoughts. I wasn't physically writing them down, but I was writing them in my mind, keeping count and score.

If you are in a negative or self-destructive state, it's important to work on your mind each day. Just five or ten minutes of giving yourself a break, not judging your behavior harshly, and simply observing your thoughts without reacting, can shift you. Self-limiting beliefs with emotional charge are creative in nature. We can't always control which thoughts arise, but we can control how we react. We can transform them. We can observe them. We can say, "Oh, there it is again."

What's interesting about destructive or self-limiting thoughts is that when you shine a light on them, they shrink away. When you react to them, they gain power. This is why Buddhists emphasize awareness of their thoughts and words.

Reality does not matter. Matter is not reality. The Kabbalists would say that this reality is the 1% and the 99% is the Spiritual reality....the true reality. I learned this also, through studying the words of Thoth and experiencing this reality through ayahuasca. This is a mental universe. Mind is frequency, sinusoidal waves, and spirals in mathematical sequences. As Pythagoras said: All is mind, and mind is number.

Try this: close your eyes and imagine a dog. Who is seeing the dog? How do you see the dog without eyes? Who created the dog in your mind? How did you simply create the dog in your mind? Who heard you ask to create the dog? The answer, of course, is you, the real you. The you who, in consciousness, can hear without ears and create images without pen and paper. Your mind imagined and created the dog. This is the creative force of everything. The All is contained in everything, and you are The All.. This is the understanding that drove me to write this book.

We are one mind, split to experience singularity and multiplicity. We are a hologram composed of zeros and ones and waves and internally connected to ourselves while asleep, and we connect to the hologram of the universe while awake. We preexist this body and live after this body has gone back to mud. You are not your body. I am not the body. You are in heaven now, dreaming that you are not here. You are always in spirit, always. Just a small sliver of you is experiencing this stream of consciousness in a body. Feel free to wake up and win the game. The physical world is a training ground for evolution.

I am not my job, my mortgage, or my rent. I am not my politics, my race, or my religion. I am not what my parents, relatives, children, or friends think I might be. I am not my bank account. I am a divine being capable of so much more than I can imagine. Jesus said, "All this and more, you will do." Imagination is your essence. I create my life, all of it.

I am the lead actor, producer, writer, and play all the parts. I am. I create.

Take this understanding and decide what you want, with courage, with power, with confidence. This is your right. This is what was intended for you in this life. You are here to create. That reflection is the image of God.

I must admit, I never could visualize the description of God in the Bible. For me, He seemed like 2 gods – one preoccupied with battle, sacrifice, and rules with harsh penalties, and the other protective, loving, and all-knowing, wisdom and power. It became easy to join the agnostic and atheist perspectives. Like Einstein, I believed in the God of Spinoza. It is clear there is elegance in the design of everything, so it didn't align with the rigid depictions I read about God. I followed thoughtful atheists and agreed: one can be moral and ethical without religion.

All of this shifted when I drank ayahuasca for the first time. I was privileged to enter the sanctuary of eternity. I found myself, my true self, in the presence of the Holy One. This was not a physical presence. At first, I thought I might choke to death, unable to swallow or breathe from the sheer intensity. Then I was enveloped in glorious wisdom, power, knowing, and infinite love. It was profoundly clear to me that, of course, this Quality could easily create all of existence. I felt the knowing. I knew it could and did create the Universe and All Universes. I had experienced and realized God.

This was not love in the usual sense of the word. To put it gently, I trembled in that presence, recognizing it as the core of my being. I wanted to lie down in supplication. I would have been honored to do so. But I was gently encouraged to join others in this dimension of majesty. They were clear that lying down in this way was not required or necessary. Just 3 things were required. An open heart, humility, and courage.

The source of peace and happiness is in you. It has always been. It is not hiding. You are precious to the Creator. I have felt this powerfully. We are all precious. We are the grandsons and granddaughters of Creation, the All. The universe is the son and daughter, with its own soul and mind. Nothing occurs that does not bring you benefit. I am here to evolve in awareness and experience.

It became obvious to me as I was disengaged from the love affair with my body that the purpose of life is not to identify with just my body. If I were to evolve, I must understand that I was going too far with my connection to just the body. I imagined that I was this body, mind, and spirit, but all it was was words. I believe that we are here to evolve to this awareness. How could cancer, failed back surgery, financial ruin, divorce, a car accident, and clinical depression be to my benefit? Easy. I simply look at my life now and what I overcame. I understood it was necessary to suffer through these experiences in order to hit rock bottom so that I could discover and live as the being behind the face. None of my contentment and happiness would have been possible without suffering, learning, and overcoming.

Ask: Who is aware? It is you. This is not difficult. It is not only for a chosen few. It is your right. We are all kings. Please allow this. It is not something to earn, it is simply something to know. Truly know.

Awakening is built into your DNA. It is for you to discover. It is inside you, and the path is to find it. Go within. All the clues are there. As Jesus said, "The kingdom of God is within."

Your path is like a fingerprint. It is not what anyone tells you it must be. Religions tell us to find God outside ourselves. They won't tell you that in your highest condition, you are God. They won't tell you that you are divine. But you are.

Chapter 20

I Am

The real purpose of this life, it seems to me is to take a bite of that apple and experience life in all its complexities: pain, suffering, joy, dying, celebrating, laughing, mourning, achieving, failing, regretting, begging, bragging, preening, bullshitting, lying, cheating, worrying, loving, hating, and finally waking up and remembering.

LIVING. EXISTING/BEING CONSCIOUSNESS, BLISS.

I would encapsulate my belief of what I am as a portion of God, the Creator of all Existence. I am this tiny self of the One Big Self. We are all selves of the One Self. I am a shard of light of the Holy Light. We are souls within the One Soul. We are a tiny mind connected to the One Mind. We are a singularity of multiplicity.

As Buddhism teaches, I am a grain of sand in the desert, therefore the desert. I am a drop of the ocean, therefore the ocean. I am a cell in the heart of God; therefore, I am God.

There is nothing made of anything but this One Self. There is nothing contained or located anywhere. It's all here, now, in this All.

I don't look for God somewhere else. I don't ask an intermediary to connect me to God. I don't need a book to give me a roadmap. As the Sufi mystics said, "God is closer than your own breath." As Jesus said, "The Kingdom of God is within."

WALK SOFTLY

I am this portion of God, I think, knowing itself through my existence and all my struggles and experiences. I remember what I am now, and that is the awakening. The Being Behind the Face. I try to walk softly now. It's not something that my personality found easily before I began to see. Everything has the quality of the Creator. I don't look for God - it's in everything.

I am never alone, so being alone is to me Holy. It's a chance to be with all of them. There is humility and courage and an open heart waiting for me in these moments.

There is Just One Self
The All

I have seen blue orbs surrounding me that came out of the sun, and then an enormous pink dragon burst out of the sun, following the orbs. I have seen the OM symbol written in the sky in gold, blue, orange and pink.

I have been awakened by the singing of an Angel imploring me to free my Tree of Life, and after a deep breath, I saw the Universe come out of my mouth, and I melded with it.

I have heard the voices of Creator gods that laughed in joy as they welcomed me into their domain. I have been in the dimension of the Creator and survived the choking and shivering and numbness and fear, and then felt its bliss and wisdom, and knowing and power and love.

I have seen the Play of the Human Being and watched the celestials look on with precious love of our courage.

I have felt the drops of anointing as they fell on my head and face.

My soul is restored, and I love God in a way that I never imagined was possible. My words can not express this. I adore Its Creations and I feel and know my portion within It.

I watch videos of animals playing with each other and loving each other. It fills my heart, and I know this is the preciousness that they ALL feel for us.

I have felt true love in the heart of God, and though I could go only so far into the eternity and infinity beyond time and space of this limitless quality, it was transforming.

I know that this is what I am. I am what I can be. I am that I am and what we can be. I burned the inauthentic self into ashes like Shiva. I created a new life and Universe like Brahma, that is now my authentic self. I preserve myself in my own embrace, like Vishnu.

I am the simulator creating my Play of this life. It's always been me. It's always been you.

Acknowledgements

There are many people who have led me to write this book and offer such a personal experience.

First, I will acknowledge the reluctance I had to strip bare my personal thoughts and experiences in my Spiritual path. Each of us has our own path, and like a fingerprint, it's uniquely ours and therefore has its own quality.

It starts with my old friend Tolo, the traveler, adventurer, lover of life, writer and psychic of the highest magnitude. He would ask me, "So when will you write and teach?" Sadly, Tolo beat me to the punch and put his own book out before me!

My Ayahuasca experiences and deep friendships made with a particular group, Mike, Tim, Ben, Chris, Brandon, Norelle and Corrado, inspired my writing with "Let me read your book when it's finished."

When I stopped writing for several months, I received a jolt of a question from Spirit: "When will you start writing again?" To say this was a powerful medicine/cure for writer's block is an understatement.

To my cousin Eileen, who first listened to my experiences and saw many supernatural pictures and even suggested, when in Kauai, to keep taking pictures (some are in the book). She read thousands of words and made dozens of suggestions, and I am grateful for her support.

To my parents, who have taught me so much about life.

To my children, who will learn quite a bit about Dad! You are my precious jewels.

To my Spirit Guides and Angels and Celestials who honored me with a connection that still seems unbelievable... but is quite believable, in fact, knowable.

To the Creator of All that resides in all of us, and is the Quality of All of Existence.

Photos from My Life

**My parents, Irv and Sonia,
together at an American Cancer Society event.
My mother was honored over a dozen times for her skilled volunteer work and leadership.**

My mother Sonia - age 22 on her wedding day

Me holding baby Rachel

Me holding baby Sean with the same screams of joy on both our faces.

Sean in 10th grade

Me buffed out at age 35, wearing too short shorts as usual.

My Uncles, Morris Silberman and Albert Reitman and my Father, Irv in WW2, met up for drinks. This picture has been revered by our large family for 80 years.

Rachel, my daughter

Additional Reading/Resources

1. Elizabeth Hatch: *Initiation*
2. Dr. Wayne W. Dyer: *Wishes Fulfilled*
3. Dr. Richard Louis Miller: *Psychedelic Medicine*
4. Florence Scovel Shinn: *The Game of Life and How To Play It*
5. Zecharia Sitchin: *There Were Giants Upon the Earth*
6. Alan Watts: *The Book: On the Taboo Against Knowing Who You Are*
7. Geshe Michael Roach: *The Diamond Cutter: The Buddha on Managing Your Business and Your Life*
8. Dr. Gerardo Sandoval: *The God Molecule*
9. Jane Leavy: Sandy Koufax
10. Jaime Meyer: *Healing with Shamanism: Practices and Traditions to Restore and Balance the Self*
11. Billy Carson: *Compendium Of The Emerald Tablets*
12. Napoleon Hill: *Think and Grow Rich*
13. Tim Freke and Peter Gandy: *The Hermetica: The Lost Wisdom of the Pharaohs*
14. Paul Gorman: *The 4 Secrets of the Universe*
15. Joel L Kraemer: *Maimonides: The Life and World of One of Civilization's Greatest Minds*
16. H. P. Blavatsky: *The Land of the Gods: The Long-Hidden Story of Visiting the Masters of Wisdom in Shambhala*
17. Steven Nadler: *Spinoza*
18. M J Evans, pHD: *Zecharia Sitchin and the Extraterrestrial Origins of Humanity*
19. Mariana Stjerna: *Agartha: The Earth's Inner World*
20. Keith Dowman: *The Flight of the Garuda: The Dzogchen Tradition of Tibetan Buddhism*
21. Garth Fowden:T*he Egyptian Hermes: A Historical Approach to the Late Pagan Mind*
22. E. A. Wallis Budge: *The Egyptian Book of the Dead: The Papyrus of Ani in the British Museum*
23. J.D. Buck: *Mystic Masonry*
24. Eknath Easwaran: *The Bhagavad Gita*
25. Manly P Hill: *The Pineal Gland: The Eye of God*
26. Akiba ben Joseph: *Sefer Yetzirah: The Book of Formation*
27. David Hawkins, MD: *The Way to God: Devotion - The Way to God Through the Heart*
28. Sripad Jagannatha Das: *Brahma Vishnu Shiva: The Yogic Trinity with the Brama Samhita*
29. Michael Newton: *Journey of Souls: Case Studies of Life Between Lives*
30. Neven Paar: *Serpent Rising: The Kundalini Compendium*
31. Thomas Egenes and Vernon Katz: *The Upanishads*
32. Paramhansa Yogananda: *How to be Happy all the Time*

Notes

The purpose of this book is to inspire you to hopefully initiate a dialogue between us. Please use these last pages to write notes that you can then email to me to begin our discussion.

To Contact Jim:
jimlowitz@gmail.com
www.thebeingbehindtheface

www.ingramcontent.com/pod-product-compliance
Ingram Content Group UK Ltd.
Pitfield, Milton Keynes, MK11 3LW, UK
UKHW062258290726
14090UKWH00017B/764